The Honey and Yoghurt Cookbook

The Honey and Yoghurt Cookbook

by Rena Cross

London: W. FOULSHAM & CO LTD

First published in Great Britain by
W. Foulsham & Co. Ltd
Yeovil Road, Slough, SL1 4JH

© W. Foulsham & Co. Ltd. 1974

All rights reserved.

ISBN 0-572-00891-0

Printed in Hong Kong

Contents

Introduction	page 7
Yoghurt	
Preparation of Yoghurt	11
Sauces, Dressings and Dips	14
Starters	17
Soups	19
Poultry	22
Meat	25
Fish	29
Main-Course Salads	32
Vegetables	34
Desserts	36
Drinks	42
Yoghurt Cheese	
Dips	43
Starters	44
Fish	46
Desserts	47
Honey	
Dressings	53
Starters	54
Meat	55
Main-Course Salads	57
Side Salads	58
Desserts	59
Bread and Cakes	61
Sweets	64
Preserves and Spreads	67
Pickles and Relishes	69

WEIGHTS & MEASURES

The following abbreviations are used throughout the book.

tbs = Tablespoon
dsp = Dessertspoon
tsp = Teaspoon
lbs = Pounds
oz = Ounce
pt = Pint

Introduction

This is not a "health food" book as health food books are generally understood, although it deals with two substances commonly classified as "health foods". The definition of a health food is rather obscure, since we can no longer confine ourselves to the premise that it is a food bought at a health food shop, because many of these shops are now forced, for survival's sake, to stock a number of products that are quite definitely outside what is considered, by those who take the benefits of food really seriously, the bounds of wise eating.

At the same time supermarkets are cashing in (quite literally) on the increasing tendency to try to eat for better health by selling yoghurt, both natural and with additional fruit, wholemeal and stone-ground flour, and other products, once the province of the health store alone. Honey has been the grocer's hardy perennial for centuries.

Thus we can no longer presume that what we buy at the health store is wholly to our benefit and that what we buy at the supermarket will offer poor nutrition and possibly actual harm. White flour, refined sugar, tea and coffee are all potentially harmful. Butter is considered to increase the blood cholesterol level and there is some evidence that margarine carries its own hazards. Cyclamates are out, saccharin may well follow. The actions of buying and eating increasingly resemble the picking of one's way through a thorny path beset with unknown hazards. Reading the list of contents on a food package is a salutary and alarming experience, unless you are a graduate in food chemistry, as it reveals, if it reveals nothing else, the paucity of our own knowledge as to what is potentially harmful. A food scare blows up, fanned by the news media; but it either dies away and is forgotten because the public has decided to eat and be damned (or because there is vested interest involved), or else it results in the withdrawal of that particular substance from the market, often on the flimsiest evidence.

Those of us who value our health are placed in constant dilemmas as to what to eat and what to avoid, and many of us may feel that safety lies only in a diet of brown rice and vegetables. Or does it? What about insecticides? What about the soil in which the rice is grown? No, we are safe with most of the world's natural foods. Insecticides are only an external hazard, removed by washing fruit, salad materials and vegetables. Growing plants are discriminating in the substances they absorb, and although artificial fertilizers render them deficient in many mineral salts that are found only in compost grown vegetables, there are few health hazards here.

Obviously you cannot fall prey to the fallacy that "nothing that grows in nature can be harmful" and make a pudding out of deadly nightshade berries, or experiment, without the aid of a good instruction book, in the eating of fungi and toadstools, even though fewer are poisonous than members of the public believe.

Meat, fish and poultry are also natural foods, although vegetarians manage very well without them. The dangers of eating today lie in the processing, preserving, denaturing, flavouring and colouring of so much of our food. When so many people tend to place convenience above safe nutrition the best that you can say for many of these foods is that they taste nice (if you like that sort of thing), are quickly prepared without the requirement of the slightest cooking ability, and do us (we hope) no actual active harm. The fact that they have lost all or most of their vitamin and mineral content during processing is considered immaterial, since we can always get a bottle of vitamin pills. . . .

It is reassuring therefore to consider two natural foods, yoghurt and honey, from which we can obtain not only safe nutrition but an extraordinary number of specific health benefits. There are no substitutes. Attempts to make synthetic honey were a failure. Yoghurt is so cheap and so easy to make that to seek a substitute would be laughable. It would also be unprofitable, which puts yoghurt at no risk of synthesization.

But as we said before, this is not a health book as health books are generally understood. It does not advocate a total honey and yoghurt diet to the exclusion of all other foods, although such a diet would be viable and in fact many yogins have survived in perfect health on it for years. It is possible to exist on honey alone for many days, in a state of contemplation and meditation, and to emerge rejuvenated, but this again is beyond the scope of this book.

Instead we present yoghurt and honey as valuable adjuncts to a good and full gastronomic life, far beyond the concept of yoghurt as a quick dessert bought at the corner store when you haven't had time to make a pudding, or of honey as something to spread on bread for the children's tea. The recipes are taken from many countries, including Turkey and India, where yoghurt and honey are part of the way of life. You can eat yoghurt or honey (or yoghurt *and* honey) in the recipes in this book every day for well over six months and never make the same dish twice.

We ourselves do not always eat yoghurt every day, although we do consume fair quantities of it. Honey is used as a basic sweetener, in tea and coffee as well as in desserts. Sugar is seldom found in the house, but we buy honey in 7 lb tins for cheapness and use it lavishly. The favourite quick snack, when pressure of work does not permit time for a meal, is yoghurt with honey. We add yoghurt to a number of dishes, including meat, poultry and fish, not because— By God, yoghurt is good for us and we're going to get it down our throats one way or another—but because yoghurt makes so many good things so very much better; it is one of life's bonuses that it does us so much good. Because, yes, it does us good, and honey does us good, physically and we believe mentally as well, since brain activity increases as energy increases. Our experiments into yoghurt- and honey-living have been vastly successful and have certainly added an extra gastronomic dimension to our lives.

Yoghurt

YOGHURT is almost as old as time and developed apparently simultaneously throughout the warmer parts of the world from the time when the milk of various animals was first utilized. Milk does not remain in its original condition for very long in hot countries, and where food is at a premium it cannot be wasted as natural changes occur. Thus yoghurt was first eaten because milk could not be wasted when the taste sharpened and the curd thickened and clotted. In spite of the fables about " the first man to discover yoghurt ", it must have been discovered almost as soon as milk was set aside rather than being consumed as soon as it was gathered from an animal. The line between fresh milk and milk that has slightly soured is a very fine one, as we all know when we add yesterday's milk to a cup of tea and wait to see if it mixes in or separates out.

But slightly soured milk is not yoghurt, only the beginning of it. The souring of milk is not a process of " turning bad " but an increase in its natural lactic bacillus, which causes slight fermentation. In these enlightened days we have gone beyond the presumption that all bacilli are harmful, and live with the idea that some are not only beneficial, but even essential to life and health, including those within our own bodies, especially the excretory system. The yoghurt bacilli have a wonderful healthful and stimulatory effect on our own internal bacilli, which makes for good general health. They also help to combat specific infections, especially various types of internal infections.

If you leave fresh milk to stand undisturbed in a warm place it will form into a soft jelly within a matter of a few days. The consistency is not unlike that of junket, but the taste is slightly sharp, instead of being bland. If you spoon into yoghurt, whey will run out of it as in junket. This is a primitive kind of yoghurt. It is very pleasant eaten with sugar or honey (though possibly a little sharp to be eaten plain) and was undoubtedly the first kind of yoghurt ever made. (Incidentally, the word " yoghurt " is the Armenian and Turkish name for the preparation and it is from these countries that it came to the western world. It is known by many other names in other parts of the world.)

The original differences in yoghurt taste would have been due to the different animals from which the milk was obtained, this being dictated by the type of husbandry practised. People in Britain are limited to milk from cows and goats simply by custom (very good goat's milk yoghurt made by the firm of Zambibwe can be obtained in many health food shops in the West of

England and the Midlands).

If you travel, particularly in the East, you will find other varieties of yoghurt beyond the simple difference in animal origin, though not all are acceptable to western tastes. These include the heavily fermented *Kefir* and *Koumiss*, which take the form of an alcoholic drink as well as a milk food and are subject to closed fermentation, usually in a goatskin bag. The taste, not entirely pleasant to westerners, comes from small masses of micro-organisms called " seeds "; these are added to a fresh brew from the previous one, much in the way that yeast is passed from one brew of beer to another.

Yoghurt in its simplest form was slow to progress to the western world, though it was eaten in quantity by immigrants from countries where it was considered a staple part of the diet. It was only after the Second World War that American grocers who supplied these immigrants with yoghurt saw the possibilities of an extended trade. But it took the addition of sugar and fruit to induce the general Western public to accept what has been an accepted dietary necessity to millions of people for thousands of years.

Yoghurt is the most easily digested and assimilated form of milk food and is absorbed three times faster than fresh milk. It is therefore extremely suitable for those who do not find fresh milk and milk products easy to digest. This applies particularly to babies and young children with a poor tolerance of fresh cow's milk. The often-quoted axiom that " milk is a perfect food " is incomplete, since milk is a perfect food only for the young animal it was intended to nourish. Therefore cow's milk is the perfect food for a sucking calf, but it should not be a matter of surprise that some human stomachs, especially baby stomachs, do not accept it readily. In yoghurt, however, the chemical changes that take place render the milk more digestible, so that it can even be given to sufferers from various intestinal complaints, including ulcerative colitis and chronic dysentery, and can form part of the diet in spastic colitis with great benefit. In introducing babies and young children to yoghurt, start by mixing one-third yoghurt with two-thirds fresh milk and gradually increase the yoghurt strength.

Those who suffer from gastric disorders, including gastric or duodenal ulcers, may tend to avoid yoghurt because they feel that it is an " acid " food, but in fact yoghurt helps to neutralize the natural hydrochloric acid in the stomach and can bring a great deal of relief. It is considered to be a specific against nausea in pregnancy and fulfils the desire for " something sour " that many women experience during pregnancy. It's also rich in calcium, which is in accordance with most pregnancy diets.

The secret of the beneficial effect of yoghurt lies in its lack of bulk and easy absorption, so that it places no strain whatsoever on the digestive system. Coupled with the fact that it is very nutritious (high in protein, vitamins and mineral salts) and that it inhibits the growth of harmful bacteria in the digestive system, it can be taken with great advantage when other foods are inadvisable. When we talk about the high digestibility of yoghurt we are talking of plain natural yoghurt, of course. If you find fruit hard to digest you will undoubtedly find fruit yoghurt easier to digest than whole fruit on its own; but when we refer to complete and easy digestibility in the case of illness we are thinking in terms of plain yoghurt.

Preparation of yoghurt

We have already discussed the simplest possible way of making yoghurt—by leaving fresh milk to stand until it sets. But there are other and better ways.

Yoghurt can be made with fresh milk, either raw or scalded, and from dried milk, again either raw or scalded. Milk is scalded by bringing it up to the boil slowly and boiling it for about one minute; use a fairly large saucepan or else it will boil over. (Remember that if you rub a little butter round the inside rim of the saucepan, it is less likely to boil over.) The scalded milk is then inoculated with natural yoghurt (bought in a carton when you are making your first batch and from your previous day's making thereafter), or with a commercial "starter", which is usually in crystal form.

The temperature of the setting yoghurt should be controlled at 65°F (18°C), so that it will be ready in the shortest possible time (about 8 hours). This greatly improves the flavour. It can be made overnight, but needs to cool for 2 or 3 hours before it is eaten, so last night's yoghurt is for *tomorrow*'s breakfast. As it keeps well in the fridge for 3 or 4 days (possibly for up to a week) this really creates no problem; you can have one lot in the making, one in the fridge and one on the table.

There are two "mechanical aids" to the making of yoghurt. Both can be bought at health food shops, one can be made at home. An electric yoghurt "machine" is extremely convenient and easy to use and costs about £4.50. The other takes the form of a covered dish, lined with insulating material, in which stand a number of small cups or wide-mouthed bottles to contain the inoculated milk. It is the function of both these aids to ensure that the milk cools as slowly as possible to allow for maximum growth of lactic bacilli.

Home-made yoghurt maker

To make your own insulated container:

1 Take a round biscuit or sweet tin with a well-fitting lid.

2 Make an insulating pad to go right round the inside, one for the bottom of the tin and one to fit inside the lid, by cutting out suitably sized pieces of stout cotton fabric, such as unbleached muslin, making covers and filling them with any good insulating material—feathers, foam rubber, kapok, upholsterer's wadding etc.

3 Place the bottom and side pads in position and fit in as many cups or wide-mouthed bottles (sterilize them first) as the tin will reasonably hold. Make sure that they are not too high for the lid to fit on properly.

4 After pouring the prepared milk into the cups or bottles (see instructions below) place a large (sterilized) cork mat on top of them, making sure that it covers all the apertures, and cover with the top pad. Close the lid firmly.

Preparing the milk

1 Scald the milk, keeping back about 3 teaspoons from each pint of milk used.

2 Pour the milk into the bottles or cups.

3 Take a teaspoonful of natural yoghurt to each pint of milk used and mix it with the milk you have kept back, and cooled.

4 When the milk in the cups or bottles drops to 108°F (42°C) (i.e. when you can comfortably dip your finger in it) divide the yoghurt/milk mixture equally between all containers, add and stir well.

5 Cover as directed above and close the lid of the tin, placing it in a temperature of not less than 65°F (18°C) for at least 8 hours or

preferably overnight.

If you are using a commercial starter, follow the directions on the bottle or packet, as these vary slightly according to the manufacturer. Commercial starters tend to be expensive (costing about 30p to make one batch of yoghurt) and are therefore viable only for your very first batch. After this you can use a few teaspoons of your previous day's making. Always keep a few teaspoons back for this purpose from any yoghurt you make. After you have been making yoghurt for about a week it will begin to "mature" and become sweeter, and the previous day's starter will give you a very good yoghurt indeed. After a certain time (the length will depend on a number of circumstances) the yoghurt will begin to sour again and you should start afresh with a commercial starter or bought natural yoghurt.

It is virtually impossible to have a failure if you inoculate the milk at the correct temperature and your tin is sufficiently insulated to maintain warmth overnight. If the milk is too hot or too cold you will find that there has been very little or no activity.

If you suspect that the yoghurt bacilli were actually killed by having the milk too hot, you can reinoculate it and proceed according to the directions. If the milk was too cold, or cooled too fast, simply move it to a warmer place and everything should proceed properly.

Sauces, Dressings and Dips

Sauce Tartare

8 fl oz natural yoghurt
8 fl oz yoghurt dressing (page 15)
1 tbs parsley ⎫
1 tbs red pepper ⎪
1 tbs green pepper ⎬ finely chopped
2 tbs sweet pickle ⎪
1 tbs chives ⎭
½ tbs celery seed

Mix all ingredients well. Serve with fish or vegetables.

Sauce Béarnaise

4 fl oz tarragon vinegar
Sprig fresh tarragon (or ½ tsp dried tarragon leaves)
1 chopped shallot
1 tsp chopped parsley
8 fl oz natural yoghurt
3 egg yolks
Salt and pepper

Combine vinegar with chopped shallot and tarragon leaves, add salt and pepper, and boil until mixture reduces to about half its original volume.

Cool and strain. If you are using fresh tarragon, chop the leaves finely and set them on one side.

Place the vinegar in the top of a double boiler, but don't allow the water in the bottom half to boil. Lightly beat the egg yolks and beat into the vinegar gradually until it thickens.

Fold in yoghurt, still beating hard; remove from heat and add chopped tarragon leaves and parsley. Serve immediately—with steak or chops.

15 Yoghurt Sauces, Dressings and Dips

Béchamel Sauce (white sauce)

1 oz flour
1½ oz butter or margarine
1 finely chopped shallot
½ pt milk
4 fl oz natural yoghurt
Blade mace
Salt and pepper to taste

Boil the milk with the mace, shallot and seasoning. Melt the butter in a saucepan and stir in the flour to make a roux. Strain the milk, adding it to the roux slowly, beating as you pour. Bring to the boil, stirring all the time, then adjust seasoning. Stir in yoghurt.
    Serve with fish, vegetables, poultry —or almost anything.

Sauce Soubise

8 fl oz béchamel sauce
6 onions, minced or finely chopped
2 oz butter or margarine
Pinch powdered sugar
2 tbs natural yoghurt

Brown the onions with a good chunk of butter in a frying pan, then add the Béchamel sauce, powdered sugar and more salt if required. Cook very slowly for half an hour and then strain. Add a few pieces of butter and the yoghurt, and stir well.
    Serve with meat, poultry, or vegetables.

Barbecue Sauce

1 small finely chopped onion
2 tbs olive oil
8 fl oz natural yoghurt
2 tbs Worcester sauce
1 clove garlic, minced
8 fl oz tomato ketchup
Chilli sauce to taste (use with caution)

Place all ingredients in a saucepan and bring slowly to the boil, stirring all the time. Simmer for 10 minutes, still stirring.
    Brush over meat while cooking over a barbecue grill.

Chilli Sauce

Take an empty "shaker" bottle, such as is used for Worcester sauce or vinegar, and pack it tight with dried hot chillies. Fill with good dry sherry and use as required. When all the sherry is used up, replenish it, because the "bite" in the chillies will remain for many a long day.

Horseradish Sauce

8 oz grated horseradish
8 fl oz natural yoghurt
1 tsp made English mustard
1 tsp castor sugar
Salt to taste

Mix all ingredients, adding the yoghurt last.
    Serve with boiled beef and cold meats. Try it with beetroot—there is a definite affinity.

Plain Yoghurt Dressing

8 fl oz natural yoghurt
Squeeze lemon juice
Salt and pepper to taste

Mix and serve on salads.

Garlic Yoghurt Dressing

Add ¼ tsp garlic salt, or juice of freshly pressed garlic, to plain yoghurt dressing.

Russian Yoghurt Dressing

Add to plain yoghurt dressing:

1 tsp finely chopped gherkin
½ tsp celery seed
1 tsp finely chopped red pepper
1 tsp finely chopped chives

Yoghurt and Honey Dressing

8 fl oz yoghurt
1 tbs honey
Juice of 1 lemon

Mix honey and lemon, then blend in yoghurt.

Yoghurt Mayonnaise

1¼ tbs cornflour
½ tsp salt
½ tsp mustard
1 tsp honey
16 fl oz water
4 fl oz vinegar
4 fl oz olive oil
2 egg yolks
4 fl oz yoghurt

Place all ingredients, except oil, egg yolks and yoghurt, into a saucepan. Cook slowly, stirring all the time, until mixture thickens. Boil for 1 minute, remove from heat and cool a little.

Beat in the egg yolks, one by one, and then beat in the oil very gradually. Chill, and add the yoghurt an hour before serving.

Yoghurt Dips

When using natural yoghurt, as opposed to yoghurt cheese (see page 42), as a dip, it is better to beat it up a bit to give it a slightly stiffer consistency.

In saying that almost *anything* can be added to yoghurt to make a dip, we obviously don't mean that you should combine dates and sardines for instance, although you would doubtless find someone to say that it was delicious, even if only out of perversity. But ingredients that are harmonious in, for instance, a salad, either fruit or vegetable or a combination of both, will go together even more harmoniously to make a dip. With a little experimentation your own particular favourites will emerge.

Crudités

These are simply prepared raw vegetables dipped into various yoghurt dressings.

Cut young carrots into sticks, and if you can get a nice young turnip cut that into sticks too. (Raw turnip has a quite different flavour from when cooked; it is spicy and not unlike a mild radish.) Include fennel (the vegetable, not the herb) if it is in season, and the sweet nutty salsify.

Cut strips of red and green pepper, chunks of celery, generous pieces of cucumber, wedges of very firm tomato. Pull a young cauliflower to pieces so that you have a series of tiny heads on a tiny stalk. Take very fresh and pink button mushrooms.

Provide toothpicks or cocktail sticks, and serve as many yoghurt dressings as you fancy, possibly including a few of the honey dressings from page 15. Serve the dressings very cold.

Waldorf Dip

2 cooking apples
1 stick celery, diced
4 oz raisins
1 tbs chopped walnuts
½ pt natural yoghurt
Salt and icing sugar to taste
Pinch curry powder
Paprika

Peel and dice apples and add immediately to yoghurt, or they will go brown. Then add celery, walnuts and raisins. Season with salt, sugar and curry powder and chill. Sprinkle with paprika just before serving.

Serve with potato chips and small cracker biscuits. (This of course applies to all dips.)

Curry Dip

½ pt natural yoghurt
1 tsp curry powder (or according to taste and brand used)
Pinch powdered cumin
½ small cucumber, finely chopped

Blend the curry powder and cumin with a small quantity of yoghurt, then add the rest, stirring well. Add chopped cucumber.

Garlic Dip

½ pt natural yoghurt
1 tsp garlic salt (or to taste)
  or juice of 2 cloves garlic
A few chopped chives
Salt and black pepper

Combine all ingredients, stirring well.

Strawberry Dip

This one may come as a surprise, but is quite delicious because it brings out the full flavour of the strawberries.

½ pt natural yoghurt
½ tsp salt
Pepper
1 lb large strawberries

Season the yoghurt fairly strongly with salt and pepper. Do not hull the the strawberries, because the hulls make good " holders " for dipping.

Tomato Dip

½ pt natural yoghurt
½ pt tomato ketchup
Garlic salt or garlic juice to taste
1 tsp French mustard
Salt and black pepper to taste
Coarsely chopped parsley

Blend all ingredients, adding parsley last.

Plum and Carrot Dip

1 lb ripe plums
½ pt natural yoghurt
1 tsp icing sugar
Carrot sticks

Skin and stone plums, mash them with the sugar and beat in yoghurt. Cut young carrots into sticks to be used as " dip sticks ", or chop them finely and add to the dip.

Starters

Waldorf Slaw

½ lb cole slaw cabbage
2 finely sliced Bramley apples
Salt water
2 oz raisins
2 oz chopped walnuts
Stick celery
Tin mandarin segments
½ pt mayonnaise (page 16)
Pinch ground ginger
Black grapes and tomato slices for
  decoration

Peel, core and finely slice apples into a bowl of salt water. Shred cabbage, place in a bowl, adding drained mandarin segments, raisins, walnuts and chopped celery. Add ground ginger to mayonnaise, season if necessary and mix into the bowl until all ingredients are well coated. Drain apple slices and mix them in.

Halve and pip grapes and decorate the top of the slaw (which looks best served in individual dishes), adding tomato slices and lettuce leaves. Serves four.

Coupe Caprice

6 oz shrimps
1 small Charentais melon
1 small green pepper
Squeeze lemon juice
Salt
1 pt natural yoghurt or yoghurt mayonnaise (page 16)
Paprika

Head, shell and devein the shrimps, unless they are already prepared. Cut melon into slices and then dice the flesh finely. Discard the seeds from the pepper and dice finely. Mix shrimps, melon and pepper, squeeze lemon juice over and sprinkle with salt. Fold carefully into yoghurt or mayonnaise and serve in coupe or cocktail glasses, sprinkled with paprika and well chilled. A few shrimps and green pepper strips can be retained for decoration. Serves six.

Eggs Florentine

12 oz frozen spinach
¼ pt natural yoghurt
4 eggs
Pinch nutmeg
Seasoning

Thaw and drain spinach, mix with yoghurt and nutmeg, season to taste. Place at the bottom of four ramekins, building it up at the sides to make " nests ". Break an egg into each nest. Bake in a medium oven (375°F, Gas Mark 5) until the eggs are set. Serves four.

Yoghurt Mousse
The thirty-two-second starter

3 fl oz natural yoghurt
Small tin beef consommé
1 tbs dry sherry
½ tsp dried dill or dill seed

Put ingredients in the blender and blend for 30 seconds. Pour into ramekins, chill until set. Serves 4.

Eggs in Jelly

½ oz plain gelatine
Large tin beef consommé
8 hard-boiled eggs, sliced
¼ pt yoghurt mayonnaise (page 16)
Few drops hot chilli sauce
Salt and pepper
Red pimento for decoration

Melt the gelatine in a couple of tablespoons of consommé in a bowl over a saucepan of boiling water. Stir in the rest of the consommé and then pour gradually into the mayonnaise, stirring all the time. Add seasoning and stir again.

Take individual cocotte dishes and place the egg slices on the bottom. Pour the consommé/mayonnaise mixture over them. As they begin to set decorate with " leaves " made with red pimento. Refrigerate until required. Serves six.

Prawn Vol-au-Vent

4 3 in vol-au-vent cases, baked
8 oz shelled prawns
½ lb sliced mushrooms
¼ pt natural yoghurt
1½ oz butter
Seasoning

Fry the mushrooms for about 3 minutes in the butter, add the prawns and cook slowly for a further 3 minutes. Add yoghurt and season to taste.

Divide the mixture between the vol-au-vent cases and place in a hot oven (400°F, Gas Mark 6) for 10 minutes.

Serve hot or cold, garnished with lettuce leaves or cress. Serves four.

Soups

COLD SOUPS

Chicken Avocado Soup

1 very ripe avocado
½ pt chicken stock, chilled
4 tbs natural yoghurt
Few drops chilli sauce
Seasoning
1 tsp chopped chives

Peel, stone and coarsely chop the avocado. Put it in the blender with the chilled stock and chives. Blend for about 20 seconds, then strain the mixture through a fairly fine sieve into a bowl. Add chilli sauce and seasoning, stir in yoghurt. Chill for at least an hour before serving. Serves two or three.

Jajik

This is considered the classic cold yoghurt soup and is met with in many parts of the world where yoghurt constitutes much of the staple diet.
1 medium cucumber
¾ pt natural yoghurt
1 tsp wine vinegar
1 tsp olive oil
Clove garlic
1 tsp fresh mint leaves, chopped
½ tsp fresh or dried fennel
½ pt cold water
Seasoning
Ice cubes

Peel the cucumber, scoop out the seeds and chop the cucumber finely, sprinkling with salt. Crush the garlic to a paste, add herbs, oil, vinegar, oil, yoghurt, in that order. Add water to make a thin cream and fold in cucumber. Chill at least 2 hours and serve in chilled plates, adding a few ice cubes. Sprinkle with fresh chopped mint. Serves four.

HOT SOUPS

Almost any soup is improved if you float a good dollop of natural yoghurt on its surface. This is especially true of tomato or watercress soup and borscht.

Borscht

½ lb raw beetroot, coarsely grated
½ lb grated raw cabbage
Medium onion, chopped
½ tbs fresh dill leaves, chopped (or parsley if you can't get dill)
Clove garlic, minced
1 potato, grated
2 pts good beef stock
2 tomatoes, chopped
2 oz butter or margarine
2 tbs vinegar
Salt and pepper to taste
Natural yoghurt

Melt the butter or margarine and cook onions slowly for 5 minutes. Add beetroot, tomato, potato and garlic, cook for 15 min in half the stock.

Add the rest of the stock, cabbage, vinegar and seasoning and simmer for another half hour.

Serve with a natural yoghurt "floater" sprinkled with finely chopped dill or parsley.

Watercress Soup

4 oz butter or margarine
2 oz flour
1 pt chicken stock
¼ pt " top of the milk " or thin cream
2 oz minced onions
3 bunches watercress
Salt and pepper to taste
Natural yoghurt

Make a roux by melting 3 oz of the butter or margarine in a heavy pan and stirring in the flour. Cook for a minute or two without colouring. Remove the pan from the heat and gradually stir in all the stock and milk or cream. Replace over heat and bring to the boil, stirring all the time. Simmer for 3 minutes and season.

Cook the onion in the remaining butter or margarine until soft but not coloured. Wash watercress well and chop coarsely, using about half the stems. Add to onions, place lid on pan and cook very slowly for about 5 minutes.

Add to the soup and put in blender until smooth, or pass through a sieve. Reheat, adjust seasoning. Serve, adding a natural yoghurt floater garnished with coarsely chopped watercress leaves. Serves four.

Peanut Butter Soup

1 oz unsalted butter
1½ oz flour
1½ pt chicken stock
6 oz peanut butter (smooth)
Pepper to taste
Chopped chicken
Natural yoghurt

Make a roux with the butter and flour, cooking for 2 minutes. Blend with half the stock and bring to the boil, stirring. Blend the rest of the stock with the peanut butter and add to the thickened stock. Add pepper to taste and simmer for 10 minutes. To serve, top with a yoghurt " floater " and sprinkle with finely chopped chicken. Serves four.

Clear Tomato Soup

2 pt clear stock
4 large ripe tomatoes
Pinch sugar
Salt to taste
1 egg
2 tbs white wine
Few drops tarragon vinegar
Squeeze lemon juice
Arrowroot to thicken
Few drops red colouring.

Pour stock into a saucepan with tomatoes, vinegar, lemon juice, sugar and salt. Bring to the boil and simmer for an hour. Strain.

Add the lightly beaten white of one egg, *and the shell*, both of which will clear the soup, a few drops of red colouring and the wine. Bring to the boil and simmer for a further 15 minutes. Moisten a clean cloth in hot water and strain the soup through it, adding about a teaspoon of arrowroot mixed in a little cold water. Reheat if necessary. Float a generous blob of natural yoghurt on top and sprinkle it with basil. Serves four.

Note This is usually a party soup and you can make it even more special by adding the following:

Beat an egg lightly, just enough to mix yolk and white, adding the pulp of half a ripe tomato, a pinch of salt, a shaking of paprika and a few drops of red colouring. Blend it, or put through a fine sieve, and pour the mixture into a well buttered deep plate, poaching it over hot water until firm. When cold turn it out and carve it into any shape you fancy—stars, clover leaves, etc. Leave in cold water until required, then warm in hot water and float on the soup.

Yoghurt Soups

Curry and Apple Soup

1 oz butter
1 onion, chopped
1½ oz flour
1 level tbs curry powder (or to taste)
1½ pt chicken stock
1½ lb Bramley apples, peeled and sliced
Squeeze lemon juice
Seasoning
Natural yoghurt

Fry the onion in the butter until soft, stir in flour and curry powder and cook for 1 minute. Add stock, apples and lemon juice and bring to boiling point, stirring all the time. Season. Serve with a yoghurt floater. Serves six.

Curry and Rice Soup

1 oz butter
1 onion, chopped
1 tbs curry powder (or to taste)
1 level tbs flour
1½ pt meat or chicken stock
2 sticks celery
2 oz long-grain rice
Natural yoghurt

Fry the onion in the butter until soft, add curry powder and cook for 2 minutes. Stir in flour and add stock. Bring to the boil, add sliced celery and rice. Simmer until rice is tender, about 15 minutes.
   Serve with yoghurt floater. Serves six.

Now a couple of fruit soups, not for everyday meals perhaps but well worth trying for special occasions.

Orange Soup

1 lb baby carrots (canned carrots can be used)
¾ pt chicken stock
1 6¼ oz tin concentrated frozen orange juice
Salt and pepper to taste
Natural yoghurt

Cook carrots and make a purée in the blender, or by passing through a sieve. Add the stock to the purée and bring to the boil. Add orange juice and heat gently until it defrosts, then simmer for 5 minutes. Season to taste.
   Serve with a yoghurt floater. Serves four.

Apple and Wine Soup

3 oz sugar
3 lb Bramley apples, peeled and diced
1 stick cinnamon
Rind of 1 lemon, zest only
Juice of 2 lemons
6 tbs dry white breadcrumbs
1 pt water
16 fl oz dry red wine
3 tbs redcurrant jelly
Pinch salt
Natural yoghurt

Bring water, sugar and salt to the boil, add apples and breadcrumbs with cinnamon and the thinly pared lemon rind (no pith). Cook, stirring occasionally, until the apples are really soft. Remove cinnamon stick and lemon rind. Blend the mixture or put it through a sieve.
   Return the mixture to the pan and add the wine, lemon juice and redcurrant jelly. Simmer, stirring all the time, until the jelly dissolves and the whole mixture is warm.
   Serve with a yoghurt floater. Serves four.

Poultry

Turkey Suprême

This is best made in a blender although it is just possible to pass the ingredients through a fine sieve. It's an excellent way of using up left-over Christmas turkey, and festive enough for a dinner party. Also makes an excellent starter.

½ lb cooked turkey
1 small onion, sliced
1 clove garlic
1 tbs tomato purée
Good pinch curry powder
Squeeze lemon juice
1 tbs apricot jam
½ pt mayonnaise
Salt and pepper
Parsley
Paprika

Blend onion and garlic for 1 minute. Heat curry powder, tomato purée, lemon juice and jam, bringing it slowly to the boil, stirring all the time. Add onions and garlic and blend until it becomes a smooth purée. Chop turkey fairly finely, season and add to purée, folding in mayonnaise. Season.

Chill overnight and garnish with paprika and parsley just before serving with green salad or rice salad. Serves two to three.

Béchamel Chicken German style

2 young chickens, jointed
2 egg yolks
2 oz stale white breadcrumbs
2 oz Parmesan cheese
1 lb butter
6 oz sliced mushrooms
½ pt béchamel sauce
½ lemon
Salt and freshly ground black pepper
½ glass dry white wine

Beat the egg yolks and dilute with 1 tbs water to each yolk. Dip the chicken joints in the egg and then in a mixture of breadcrumbs and grated Parmesan. Melt the butter in a skillet, and when hot lay the joints in the pan, cooking until brown on all sides. Lower the heat and cook covered until almost tender. Remove the lid and add mushrooms, frying for a few minutes.

Add Béchamel sauce and lemon juice, season to taste and simmer for about 10 minutes, adding the white wine just before serving. Serves four.

Chicken Soufflé

This is one of those dishes that looks splendidly impressive and yet is extremely easy to make. It can be made from any left-over poultry, including that Christmas turkey that goes on and on and never seems to be wholly consumed. The recipe is basic, the quantities more or less up to you—according to the amount of poultry meat available.

Cooked poultry, diced
Mayonnaise
Aspic jelly

Marinate the poultry meat in mayonnaise diluted with a little milk, for 3 hours, turning frequently. Make the aspic jelly, colouring it a little if you like, and whip it to a froth. Chill a straight-sided bowl and pour a layer of whipped aspic into the bottom. Add a layer of poultry meat and then a layer of aspic.

Continue to layer aspic and poultry until the dish is almost full, then tie a stiff paper "collar" around the top of the dish so that you can continue layering, ending with a deep layer of aspic.

Chill for at least 2 hours. Remove the paper collar and serve with salad.

Creamed Chicken

1 lb cold cooked chicken, diced
16 fl oz Béchamel sauce
Pinch celery salt
Seasoning
Garnish

Mix all ingredients and cook in a double saucepan for 30 minutes. Garnish with parsley and anything colourful, such as tomato or pimento slices. This is a nice dish, but tends to look insipid unless dressed up a little. Serves four.

Chicken and Potato Pie

1 chicken, cooked
6 large potatoes, cooked
1 oz butter
2 fl oz natural yoghurt
1 egg
6 bacon or ham slices
Seasoning

Cut the chicken into small pieces. Mash the potatoes, season, add butter, beaten egg, yoghurt and beat until light and fluffy. Lightly fry bacon.

Butter a fire-proof dish and place a layer of mashed potato at the bottom, then layer chicken, potato, ham or bacon, potato, etc., until the ingredients are used up, finishing with mashed potato.

Smooth the top and bake in a moderate oven for about 45 minutes.

Cheese can be grated over the top before baking, or you can glaze the top with an egg 10 minutes before serving. Serves six.

Note: This is, of course, an excellent "left-over chicken" recipe, and the amount of the other ingredients can be reduced accordingly. Too great a ratio of mashed potato to meat will make a very, very dull dish.

Turkey Club Sandwich

A quick and substantial lunch or supper dish, not to be despised because of the ease of preparation.

For each sandwich:
¼ lb chopped cooked turkey
3 bacon rashers, fried crisp
½ tomato
1 tbs mayonnaise
3 slices toast
Lettuce

Spread one piece of toast with mayonnaise, add turkey and lettuce. Top with another slice of toast spread with mayonnaise, add bacon and tomato. Spread third piece of toast with mayonnaise and complete sandwich.

Indian Boiled Chicken

If you think that boiled chicken is a "nothing" dish, try this traditional Indian recipe. The bird can be stuffed with bacon and peppercorns, or with the stuffing recipe given below, which incidentally is also delicious with roast chicken.

This recipe is excellent if having bought your bird you feel that it may turn out to be tough and tasteless, because using this method the flavour is intensified and none of it lost. (But you won't get the traditional chicken broth out of it.)

For one chicken make stuffing as follows:
½ lb rice
3 tbs butter
3 tbs natural yoghurt
2 onions, finely chopped
5 black peppercorns
3 cardamoms (cracked)
1 tbs raisins
Salt

Fry the rice in half the butter until a light golden brown, add a little water and cook until soft and dry. Fry the onions in the rest of the butter and mix in other ingredients.

Stuff the chicken. Make a stiff dough with 1 lb plain flour and enough water to mix, rolling it out 1 in thick. Completely encase the chicken in it so that there are no cracks or crevices.

Dip a cloth in hot water, sprinkle it with flour, place the chicken in the centre and tie it up loosely. Boil for 1 hour.

To serve, remove the dough. Serves four to six, according to the size of the bird.

Game Hens

This recipe is suitable for small chickens, as well as for the smaller type of game.

3 tbs melted butter
2 tbs natural yoghurt
½ tsp rosemary
½ tsp thyme
½ tsp cracked black pepper
Salt to taste

Mix all ingredients. Halve the birds and place in an oven dish, flesh side up. Brush with the mixture and place uncovered in a moderate oven for 30 minutes, brushing with the mixture at least twice. Cover and bake until the birds are tender, probably another 30 minutes, but this depends upon the size of the birds.

Stuffed Marrow

Another "left-over" recipe in which any kind of poultry can be used.

1 large marrow
Chopped chicken
½ lb cooked rice
1 egg
1 tbs butter
1 bay leaf
2 cardamoms (cracked)
2 cloves
8 fl oz natural yoghurt
Chopped parsley
Salt and pepper

Peel and remove seeds from the marrow. Mix rice, chicken and spices and stuff the marrow, tying back the cut end with fine cotton or dental floss. Simmer gently in the yoghurt until the marrow is tender. (It will make its own juice.)

When the marrow is cooked strain off the juice and thicken with a roux of flour and butter to which the yolk of the egg is added, heat the sauce gently, stirring. Pour over the marrow before serving. Serves four.

Tandoori Chicken

1 chicken, quartered
MARINADE
½ pt natural yoghurt
Piece root ginger
2 cloves garlic
2 tsp curry powder
¼ tsp cumin
Few drops hot chilli sauce
Black pepper

Prepare the marinade by putting all ingredients (except chicken) into the blender and blending until smooth. If you haven't a blender, pound the ginger, garlic and cumin to a smooth paste, adding yoghurt and seasonings.

Skin the chicken pieces and make a few cuts in the flesh with a sharp knife for the marinade to penetrate. Rub with mixture and marinade for at least 8 hours, turning the chicken pieces occasionally.

Heat the grill to its maximum, shake the chicken pieces, but do not wipe them. Put under the grill until brown, turning once. Then lower the grill heat right down and cook until tender, about 35 minutes.

Serve with rice and chutney. Serves four.

Meat

Boeuf Stroganoff

2 lb round steak
Flour
2 tbs olive oil
2 tbs tomato purée
½ lb button mushrooms
1 tbs brandy
½ pt natural yoghurt
Salt and black pepper

Cut the steak into matchstick pieces and dredge with flour. Heat the oil in a heavy frying pan and cook onion until soft but not coloured. Add meat, tomato purée and seasoning and cook for 5 minutes. Add thinly sliced mushrooms and cook for a few minutes more. Add brandy and yoghurt and heat up again slowly. Serves four to six.

Lamb Chop Skillet

4 lamb chops
4 tomatoes
4 fl oz dry white wine
4 fl oz yoghurt
Seasoning
Good pinch fresh basil

Brown the chops on both sides in a skillet or deep frying pan, using a little butter or cooking oil. Add tomatoes, whole or cut into quarters, and cook, covered, very slowly until the chops are almost done. Add wine and yoghurt and season with pepper, salt and basil, simmering for another 10 minutes. Serves four.

Indian Pillau

This is a traditional dish, well worth the trouble of preparation. Mangoes are obtainable in this country, but tend to be expensive: one will suffice. Do not, in the interests of economy, substitute mango chutney!

2 lb lean mutton
2 lb rice
½ lb butter
1 orange
4 oz ripe mango, cut in pieces
Few white grapes, peeled and seeded
¼ lb blanched shredded almonds
¼ lb pistachio nuts, shredded
1½ pt natural yoghurt
2 large onions, thinly sliced
1 oz garlic
1 oz green ginger
1 tsp coriander
4 white peppercorns
5 cloves
5 cardamom seeds
Pinch saffron
Salt

Dice the mutton. Wash the rice well and steep it in cold water for half an hour. Pound the garlic, ginger, coriander, peppercorns, cloves and cardamoms and mix well together. Place butter, onion and meat in a pan, add yoghurt and pounded spice mixture and heat slightly until the butter melts. Add salt to taste. Mix well and place drained raw rice on top.

Soak the saffron in a little water and pour it over the centre of the rice, sprinkling the nuts, grapes, mango and quartered orange on top. Place over a brisk heat for 10 minutes, making sure it doesn't burn, then cook very slowly until the meat and rice are cooked, about 20 minutes. Serves six.

Moussaka

1½ lb minced lamb shoulder (lean)
4 aubergines
Medium tin tomato juice
1 lb onions
1 clove garlic
1 oz flour
½ tsp mixed herbs
Seasoning
Cooking oil

TOPPING
1 egg
¼ pt natural yoghurt
Seasoning

Slice the unpeeled aubergines very thinly. Sprinkle liberally with salt and leave for 30 minutes, then drain off the liquid.

Chop onions and mince the garlic. Fry the aubergine slices in an absolute minimum of oil until golden brown on both sides, then drain on kitchen paper. Fry the onions, garlic and meat in 1 tbs oil for about 10 minutes, blend in the flour, add tomato juice and herbs and season to taste. Bring to boil, stirring all the time.

Take a fire-proof dish and layer with aubergine, then meat. Continue layering, finishing with aubergine. Pour over enough liquid to moisten.

Make a custard by beating the egg and mixing in the yoghurt and seasoning. Pour it over the moussaka and bake at 375°F (Gas Mark 5) for about 45 minutes, or until the custard is set. Serves six.

Note: It is quite possible to substitute sliced potato for the aubergine, in which case the herb flavouring should be increased, and the mixture would be the better for the addition of sliced tomato.

Turkish Lamb

Shoulder of lamb, boned
2 lamb's kidneys
2 cloves garlic
Piece green ginger
Good shaking chilli sauce
1 pt natural yoghurt
Juice of 1 lemon
Seasoning
2 oz pistachio nuts
4 oz raisins
1 oz almonds
4 oz butter or margarine
1 tbs clear liquid honey
1 lb rice
Few cardamom seeds (cracked)
Stick cinnamon

MARINADE
Slash the flesh of the lamb to allow the marinade to penetrate. Prepare the marinade as follows:
Pound or blend garlic and ginger, add the chilli sauce, ½ pt yoghurt and lemon juice, seasoning to taste. This will make a paste which should be spread over the shoulder of lamb, both inside and out. Leave overnight.

STUFFING
The following day simmer the kidneys in a minimum of water until cooked and then chop. Chop the nuts, mixing them with kidneys and juice and adding the raisins, reserving a few nuts and raisins to use with the rice. Season and add enough yoghurt to make a stiff paste. Stuff the inside of the shoulder, pressing the stuffing in tight.

ROASTING
Roll the shoulder, skewer it and tie with string. Put it in a large deep casserole with the butter or margarine and place the lid on the casserole. Cook in a medium oven for an hour, then turn the meat and pour the honey over, cooking for a further 2 hours (or until tender) basting frequently with the juices.

RICE
Boil rice. Fry remaining almonds and raisins in butter or margarine with the cardamom seeds and cinnamon stick (which should afterwards be removed) and add to the rice.

SERVING
Put meat on a warmed dish, remove string and skewers and surround with rice. Skim the juice and serve separately, thickening it with arrowroot if you feel inclined. Serves six at least. A very rich dish!

Kidneys à la Turque

6 lambs' kidneys
1 onion
½ oz butter or margarine
Flour
1 pt rich stock
1 tbs dry sherry
Chopped parsley
Few drops chilli sauce
Salt and pepper
4 fl oz natural yoghurt
Boiled rice

Prepare kidneys by skinning, coring and cutting them in halves lengthways. Chop onion and fry in butter or margarine for a few minutes until soft. Add kidneys and cook them on both sides for 2 minutes.

Thicken stock with flour, bring to the boil, stirring all the time, add sherry and seasoning and simmer until thick.

Put kidneys and onions in a casserole, pour over thickened stock and put on the lid or cover with foil. Cook for about 2½ hours in a cool oven (275°F, Gas Mark 1). Stir in yoghurt. Pile a mound of rice in the centre of a dish and place kidneys around it. Garnish with parsley and serve with green salad. Serves four.

Lamb Kebabs

Kebabs (also known as shashlik) are quite easy to prepare and fun to do. They'll look attractive if you have some of those little ornamental swords, but metal skewers will do just as well.

2 lb leg of lamb (fillet end)
4 small firm tomatoes
1 green pepper
2 small aubergines
Bay leaves
Seasoning

MARINADE
1 tbs olive oil
Juice of ½ lemon
1 tbs natural yoghurt

Prepare marinade by mixing ingredients. Cut meat into small even chunks and marinade for at least 5 hours, turning occasionally.

Cut the tomatoes in half, the pepper into pieces. Slice the aubergine very thinly. Thread the meat and vegetables on to skewers, with one or two bay leaves on each skewer. Season to taste and place each kebab under the grill, turning as necessary, grilling until the meat is tender.

Serve on a bed of rice. The food is normally stripped off the skewer by the eater before tackling it.

Note: The making of kebabs admits of a great amount of variation. Mushrooms for instance are excellent, as are kidneys. All that is required of the ingredients is that they should hold together on the skewer when cooked. You might also like to try adding various herbs to the marinade.

Barbecue Pork Chops

4 pork chops
4 fl oz barbecue sauce (page 15)

Brush the chops on one side with the barbecue sauce and place under a hot grill, sauce side up. After a few minutes turn the chops and brush the other side with sauce, returning them to the grill. Continue turning and brushing on sauce until the chops are done, about 20 to 30 minutes.

Note: Pork sausages are especially delicious cooked this way.

Liver with Yoghurt and Sherry

1½ lb calves' liver, sliced
4 tbs seasoned flour
2 oz butter
8 fl oz natural yoghurt
2 tbs sherry
Salt
Paprika
Freshly milled black pepper

Flour the liver. Melt the butter in a deep pan and fry the liver for 2 minutes on each side. Add yoghurt, sherry and seasoning. Heat, stirring, until the liver is tender, but do not allow it to boil. Serves four to six.

Oslo Chops

8 neck of lamb chops
Seasoned flour
8 fl oz stock
2 dsp wine vinegar
2 dsp tomato purée
2 dsp natural yoghurt
1 dsp honey
1 tsp Worcester sauce
2 tsp Marmite
2 onions, sliced

Coat chops with seasoned flour and brown on both sides. Mix all other ingredients (except onions) and pour over the browned chops in a fire-proof dish. Slice onions on top, season if necessary. Cover the dish and bake at 400°F (Gas Mark 6) until boiling, then reduce to simmering temperature (300°F, Gas Mark 2) for 1½ to 2 hours. Serves four.

Note: Spare ribs can be cooked in the same fashion.

Fish

Plaice Duxelle

1½ lb small plaice fillets
DUXELLE
2 oz breadcrumbs
½ tsp marjoram or oregano
½ tsp chopped fresh parsley
Zest of ½ lemon
Seasoning
Milk to mix

SAUCE
Fish stock
Milk
½ oz butter
½ oz flour
2 level tbs yoghurt mayonnaise
Seasoning

Remove the dark skin from the plaice. Mix the duxelle and spread it generously on the skinned side of the plaice. Butter a pie dish and arrange the fillets on it, covering it with foil. Place it over a saucepan of boiling water and steam for about 15 minutes until the fish is tender. Keep the fish warm.

Drain off the fish stock, making it up to ½ pt with the milk. Make a roux with the butter and flour, stirring in the stock/milk mixture. Bring to the boil, stirring, and cook for 3 minutes. Stir in mayonnaise and season to taste.

Pour the sauce over the fish and serve. Serves four.

Cod en Papillote

The term *en papillote* merely means "in a parcel". This is one of the tastiest ways to cook fish, as it literally stews in its own juice and none of the flavour is lost.

4 cod steaks
2½ oz butter
1 onion, chopped
8 oz button mushrooms, sliced
2 large tomatoes, skinned and sliced
4 tbs natural yoghurt
Pinch thyme
Seasoning

Take four pieces of kitchen foil each large enough to "parcel" up a single cod steak and butter generously on one side, laying a cod steak on each buttered side.

Fry the onion in the remaining butter for 2 to 3 minutes. Add mushrooms and fry for a further minute. Cover the fish with this mixture, adding tomato, seasoning, and 1 tbs of yoghurt to each. Sprinkle with thyme. Bring the edges of the foil together and fold it over along all edges to make a loose parcel. Bake on a baking tray at 375° (Gas Mark 5) for about 35 minutes. Unwrap and serve. Serves four.

Russian Haddock

1 lb fresh haddock steaks or fillets
2 tbs seasoned flour
4 oz butter
4 oz mushrooms, sliced
2 oz plain flour
2 hard-boiled eggs, sliced
8 fl oz natural yoghurt
1 oz grated cheddar
Garnish

Cut fish into small slices, cover with seasoned flour and fry in butter for 10 minutes. Remove from pan and drain.

Fry the mushrooms in the same fat until soft. Stir in plain flour and add yoghurt gradually, stirring all the time. Season and heat right through.

Layer the fish and hard-boiled eggs in a flat fire-proof dish and pour the sauce over. Sprinkle with grated cheese and brown under a hot grill.

Garnish with parsley, sliced tomato, lemon slices etc. Serves four.

Tuna and Cucumber Flan

8 oz shortcrust pastry (to line a 7 in flan tin)
1 tin tuna fish
½ small cucumber
4 tbs mayonnaise
4 fl oz natural yoghurt
3 level tsp powdered gelatine
Water to mix
2 tsp apple cider vinegar
Seasoning

Grease the flan tin lightly, line with pastry and bake blind. Flake the tuna. Cut the cucumber into very small cubes, reserving enough to slice for decoration. Mix tuna and cucumber cubes with mayonnaise and yoghurt and spoon into the cooled flan case. Dissolve the gelatine in a little hot water to which the vinegar has been added. As it begins to set pour it over the filled flan.

Garnish with sliced cucumber, and serve with green salad. Serves four.

Baked Coley Fillets

Don't despise the formerly humble coley because it's reasonably priced. It's a very good fish and here is an excellent way of cooking it.

2 lb coley fillets
1 pt natural yoghurt
1 packet onion soup
2 tbs butter
6 mushrooms, sliced
Juice of 1 lemon
Parsley and lemon slices for garnish

Generously butter the inside of a fire-proof dish and spoon in enough yoghurt to cover the bottom. Place in a layer of fish, adding a squeeze of lemon juice. Add a layer of yoghurt sprinkled with the soup powder, then a layer of mushrooms, yoghurt and soup powder again. Continue layering in this fashion, ending with yoghurt and soup powder. Cover and bake for 20 minutes at 350°F (Gas Mark 4). Uncover and continue to bake for an extra 10 minutes.

Serve with parsley sprigs and lemon slices. Serves four to six.

Crab Casserole

1 lb chopped crabmeat
½ lb dry white breadcrumbs
8 fl oz evaporated milk (unsweetened)
8 fl oz mayonnaise
6 hard-boiled eggs, chopped
Seasoning

Butter breadcrumbs (melt knob of butter and stir in dry white breadcrumbs). Combine all other ingredients and place in buttered fire-proof dish. Top with buttered breadcrumbs and bake at 340°F (Gas Mark 4) for 20 minutes. Serves four.
Note: Prawns, shrimps or lobster can also be used.

Yoghurt *Fish*

Orange Plaice

This delicious fish dish, fancy enough to be used as a starter, is quite easy enough to make a rather special everyday summer meal, especially if served with a substantial green salad.

8 small plaice fillets (other fish can be used)
2 oranges
¼ pt mayonnaise
Watercress

Prepare the mayonnaise first, preferably the day before as the flavour develops with keeping.

Grate the rind of the oranges, making sure that no pith is included, and squeeze the juice from one half of an orange. Reserve the rest for slicing. Mix juice and peel with the mayonnaise.

Remove the dark skin from the plaice and roll up the fillets, placing them on a buttered pie plate. Cover and steam over a saucepan of boiling water until tender (10 to 20 minutes according to size).

Arrange the cooled fillets on a serving dish, coat with mayonnaise and place the orange slices around the edge of the dish. Garnish with watercress and serve with salad. Serves four.

Tuna Fish Casserole with Cashew Nuts

1 tin tuna fish, drained
½ head celery, chopped
4 spring onions or 1 tbs chives, chopped
4 tbs butter
Small tin mushroom soup
8 fl oz natural yoghurt
¼ lb cashew nuts
Chinese noodles

Sauté onions (or chives) and celery in butter, add soup, tuna and yoghurt. Place in a fire-proof dish and bake with the cover on for 30 minutes at 350°F (Gas Mark 4).

Meanwhile half cook the noodles in salted water and drain well. Spread the noodles over the fish mixture, sprinkle with cashews, either whole or chopped, and bake for another 15 minutes, reducing heat slightly. Serves four.

Kipperee

4 oz long-grain rice
2 kipper fillets (you can use the boil-in-the-bag kind)
1 oz butter
1 oz flour
½ pt milk
¼ pt natural yoghurt
2 hard-boiled eggs
Seasoning

Cook the rice and drain well, making sure the grains are separate. Cook the kippers. Melt the butter in a saucepan, add the flour and cook for a minute without browning. Remove from heat and gradually stir in milk and yoghurt. Bring to the boil, stirring all the time, and cook for a couple of minutes more. Add chopped hard-boiled egg and then the cooked rice. Season to taste.

Serve out the rice and top with the kipper fillets. Serves two or three.

Main-Course Salads

Chicken Salad

1 lb chicken, diced
2 apples, diced
1 stick celery, diced
3 hard-boiled eggs, sliced
3 chopped gherkins
Mayonnaise
Lettuce
Boiled new potatoes
Chopped chives

Mix diced chicken, apples, celery and gherkins. Season and moisten with mayonnaise. Garnish with slices of hard-boiled egg and chopped chives.
  Serve with lettuce leaves and boiled new potatoes. Serves four.

Stuffed Egg Salad

2 hard-boiled eggs per person
2 tbs grated cheese
Mayonnaise
Salt, pepper, made mustard
Paprika
Lettuce
Sliced tomatoes

Shell the eggs and slice them across in halves. Remove the yolks and pound them with a wooden spoon. Add cheese, seasoning and enough mayonnaise to moisten. Cut a tiny slice from the bottom of each egg half so that it stands up firmly. Pile the yolk/cheese mixture into the egg halves and dust with paprika. Serve on lettuce with tomato slices.

Danish Herring Salad

4 whole pickled herrings
1 small onion, sliced

MARINADE
3 tbs cherry brandy
1 level tbs tomato purée
1 tsp French mustard
1 tsp Worcester sauce

GARNISH
Capers
Finely chopped onion
Thick mayonnaise

Mix ingredients for marinade, whisking briskly. Cut the herrings into chunks, add sliced onion and leave in marinade overnight.
  Drain, divide between four individual dishes, spooning over a small amount of marinade. Decorate with mayonnaise, possibly piped through a forcing bag. Sprinkle with chopped onion and a few capers. Serve with plain green salad. Serves four.

Prawn Salad

Layer diced cooked vegetables in a ring mould and fill the mould with mayonnaise aspic (page 53). When firm, turn out the mould and fill the entire centre of the ring with dressed prawns, moistened with mayonnaise. Garnish with sliced gherkin and/or leaves cut from pimento.
Note: Salmon or other flaked fish can be used instead of prawns.

Yoghurt Main-Course Salads

Smoked Haddock Salad

8 oz cooked smoked haddock
½ cucumber
2 Bramley apples
1 tbs lemon juice
¼ pt mayonnaise
¼ pt whipped natural yoghurt
Good pinch curry powder
Salt and pepper

Skin and flake fish. Peel and dice cucumber and apples; sprinkle with lemon juice. Combine all ingredients and season to taste. Serve with lettuce and garnish as you will, possibly with decoratively cut pieces of cucumber peel, lemon slices, etc.

Cucumber Jelly Salad

1 packet lemon jelly
Hot water
1 tbs wine vinegar
8 fl oz mayonnaise
½ lb yoghurt cheese (page 42)
1 stick celery, finely chopped
1 large cucumber, diced
4 oz chopped walnuts
Seasoning

Make the jelly with rather less hot water than usual. As it starts to set mix in the other ingredients well. Leave to set and serve with lettuce and sliced tomatoes. Serves four.

Chicken Mould

1 tbs unflavoured gelatine
3 tbs cold water
6 fl oz chicken stock, boiling
6 fl oz mayonnaise
¾ lb diced cooked chicken
Seasoning

Soften the gelatine in the cold water and then dissolve it in the chicken stock. As it begins to set beat it until it is frothy, then fold in the mayonnaise and diced chicken. Season to taste. Serve with green salad. Serves four.

Spinach Salad

You may not have considered the use of raw spinach as a salad ingredient, but life is full of surprises! Choose young fresh spinach, preferably the type known as Poor Man's spinach, in which case discard the thick stalk.

1 lb spinach leaves, washed and dried
1 onion, sliced
1 stick celery, diced
4 hard-boiled eggs, sliced
Salt and freshly milled black pepper
Garlic salt
8 fl oz mayonnaise
8 fl oz natural yoghurt

Tear the spinach leaves in small pieces and place in salad bowl. Add onion, celery and eggs. Sprinkle with salt and pepper. Dilute the mayonnaise with yoghurt, adding the garlic salt, and pour over the salad. Yoghurt cheese, broken into chunks, makes a very welcome addition. Serves four.

Shrimp Loaf Salad

1 tin tomato soup
1 tbs plain gelatine
4 fl oz cold water
6 oz yoghurt cheese
8 fl oz mayonnaise
1 green pepper, finely chopped
1-2 sticks celery, chopped
1 lb fresh or tinned shrimps or prawns

Soak gelatine in cold water, then dissolve in the hot tomato soup. As it begins to set blend in mayonnaise and yoghurt cheese, then add the other ingredients, mixing well. Place in a wetted mould of any shape you fancy. Prepare a platter covered with lettuce and turn out the salad on to it. Garnish in any way you like, but it's a very good-looking dish on its own! Serves six.

Vegetables

Jacket Potatoes

Large potatoes
1 tbs natural yoghurt for each potato
Chopped chives
Salt and pepper
Paprika

Scrub and dry potatoes of equal size. Bake in a moderate oven between half and one hour according to size, until they feel soft inside when pinched.
   Chop chives and add to the yoghurt. Season. When the potatoes are ready put each in a cloth and pinch it until it splits (cutting makes the potato waxy). Spoon in the yoghurt and sprinkle with paprika.

Broccoli in Yoghurt Sauce

Fresh or frozen broccoli
Natural yoghurt, warmed
1 tsp made mustard
Salt and pepper to taste

Mix yoghurt with mustard and add seasoning. Cook and drain broccoli and pour yoghurt over.

Green Beans and Almonds

Cook frozen or prepared fresh runner or French beans. Split whole almonds lengthways (about 2 oz to ½ lb beans) and fry them in butter or margarine, turning constantly, until golden brown and crisp. Mix with the cooked beans and top with a generous dollop of yoghurt mayonnaise.

Polish Beetroot

2 lb cooked beetroot
½ onion
1 dsp butter or margarine
1 dsp flour
4 tbs milk
1 tsp grated horseradish
Salt, pepper and sugar to taste
1 tbs vinegar
Yoghurt mayonnaise or natural yoghurt

Grate the beetroot. Chop the onion and fry in butter or margarine until soft, then add the flour and cook until slightly brown. Add milk and bring to the boil. Add the rest of the ingredients, except mayonnaise, and simmer for about 6 minutes. Pour into a warmed vegetable dish and add a dollop of yoghurt mayonnaise or natural yoghurt.

Salsify

The old-fashioned name for this vegetable is "oyster plant" and it comes in the form of a long thin root with a little tuft of shoots on top. Delicate in flavour, crunchy and nutty, it can be eaten raw in salads. To cook, scrub well and boil in water, with the skin still on, for about 20 minutes. Remove skin after cooking. Serve with a generous dollop of yoghurt and honey dressing.

Cabbage

The humble cabbage, which should *not* be overcooked (shred and cook in a minimum of water with a knob of lard or cooking fat), is much better for a dressing of plain yoghurt containing a few caraway seeds.

Broad Beans à la Turque

This dish is best made with fresh broad beans, but can at a pinch be made with the dried variety if they are well soaked overnight. Served with rice it is virtually a meal on its own. It also goes well with fish.

6 fl oz natural yoghurt
1 lb broad beans
Knob butter
1 egg yolk
1 clove garlic
Freshly milled black pepper
Salt

Boil and shell the beans. Put into a thick saucepan, add yoghurt, garlic, butter and seasoning and warm through, stirring all the time. Add egg yolk and continue warming and stirring until the mixture thickens.

Stuffed Green Peppers

Again a potential meal on its own, but an excellent accompaniment to cooked ham.

4 large green peppers
STUFFING
Seasoning
4 oz minced cooked chicken
4 oz minced cooked ham
1 onion, minced
2 oz mushrooms, finely chopped
Good pinch oregano
Stock to moisten

TOPPING
¼ pt natural yoghurt
1 egg
Level tsp English mustard

Prepare the peppers by cutting off the stalk end and scooping out the seeds and core. Drop them in boiling water and leave them there for 10 minutes. Drain and cool immediately by running cold water on them. Combine stuffing ingredients, making a stiff mixture, and press well down inside the peppers. Place the stuffed peppers in a greased oven dish and bake at 375° (Gas Mark 5) for 45 minutes.

Beat together egg, mustard and yoghurt and spoon the mixture over the peppers. Cook for 20 minutes, or until the topping is set. Garnish with parsley sprigs and/or a sprinkling of paprika. Serves four.

French Beans with Pears

1 lb French or runner beans
1½ lb cooking pears (windfalls will do very well)
¾ pt stock
Small piece lemon peel
4 rashers fat bacon
1 tbs honey
1 tbs yoghurt

Peel and core the pears, and slice thickly. Drop into boiling stock with the lemon peel and simmer for 20 minutes. String and slice beans and add to pears, cooking for 20 minutes. Remove rind from bacon, and chop into small pieces, frying gradually until crisp. Remove bacon from pan and add honey to bacon fat, cooking for a few minutes. Add yoghurt and a little of the stock in the pot, returning the mixture to the pot and stirring it well in. Continue cooking, uncovered, until the liquid reduces and the pears are tender. Season well and serve sprinkled with black pepper and with the bacon scattered on the top.

Desserts

Pavlova

This is almost a national dessert in Australasia, good to eat and festive to look upon. But the combination of sweet meringue and sweet filling is a bit overwhelming to many tastes, and the alternative fillings of either yoghurt or yoghurt cheese reduces this excess sweetness and makes the dessert even more delicious. Serves four.

MERINGUE
4 egg whites
8 oz castor sugar
1 tsp vanilla essence
1 tsp vinegar
2 level tsp cornflour

Draw an 8 in circle on a piece of greaseproof or other non-stick paper and place it on a baking sheet.

Beat the egg whites until they stand up in peaks; continue beating, gradually adding the sugar until the mixture is very stiff. Continue beating, gradually adding vanilla, vinegar and cornflour.

Spread the mixture over the paper circle, and pipe (using a forcing bag, or a paper bag with a fairly large corner torn off) a built-up edge to make a flat-bottomed "nest". Place low down in the oven, which should be at the lowest possible setting, a drying rather than a cooking heat, for about an hour, until the meringue is cooked but not coloured. Cool on a wire rack. When cool turn it over carefully and remove the paper.

FILLINGS
Fill with fruit yoghurt, saving some whole or sliced fruit for decoration. Strawberries are traditional, but this is purely a matter of taste. Chinese gooseberries (now rather horribly known as Kiwi Fruit) are excellent. Tamarillos (New Zealand Tree Tomatoes) are also very good, but rather astringent, and should be sweetened. Yoghurt cheese has an affinity with most fruits and can be used as an alternative filling. An extra suggestion—chopped preserved ginger.

Strawberries Antigua

½ lb strawberries
Castor sugar
Large block vanilla ice cream

SAUCE
Peel and juice of 1 large orange
2 tsp cornflour
2 tsp clear liquid honey
Small knob butter

Hull, wash and chill strawberries. Prepare the sauce by blending cornflour with orange juice, adding more water to make ¼ pt and cooking for 3 minutes after it comes to the boil, stirring continually. Add honey, orange zest and butter, stirring well. Cool and chill.

Chill a dessert bowl and place the ice cream in it. Top with strawberries and pour the sauce over. Sprinkle with sugar. Serves four.

Apple Strudel

There is nothing difficult in making apple strudel but there is a trick to it, and the preparation of strudel pastry is time-consuming. It must be paper-thin and virtually transparent, or all you will achieve will be a rather bulky apple roly-poly.

In preparing strudel pastry you need a large working surface, because you will go far beyond the area of your pastry board. It's no good thinking that you can simply roll it out thinly enough with a rolling pin, though this is the right way to start. Once you have rolled the pastry as thin as possible beat it all over with the side of your fist so that it spreads evenly. Alternate this with careful stretching out of the edges, taking great care not to tear it. But the most important thing is the beating. You will be amazed to see a comparatively small piece of pastry spread and spread over a really enormous area.

You may end up with a sore fist, but your sense of achievement will be great!

Strudels, an Austrian dish, are not confined to apple fillings any more than choux pastry is confined to chocolate éclairs. Once you have learned the strudel technique you can make a series of quite delicious desserts, including apple and apricot, cherry and almond, plum and apple, apple and raspberry, or any fruit or combinations of fruits you fancy, as long as they are not too soft and pulpy.

Since the fillings are usually rather sweet, strudels are enormously improved if served with a lavish quantity of whipped natural yoghurt.

STRUDEL PASTRY
11 oz plain flour
1 egg, beaten
1 tbs cooking oil
½ tsp salt
Warm water to mix

Sift the flour and salt, add beaten egg, oil and warm water. Mix to a pliable paste, turn onto a floured board and knead until smooth. Turn a polythene bag inside out and flour the surface well. Turn the bag out again and place the pastry inside it, setting it aside in a warm place.

FILLING
2 lb Bramley apples
4 oz raisins
6 oz castor sugar
½ tsp cinnamon
Small pinch powdered cloves
2 oz butter
Icing sugar
Natural yoghurt topping

Peel and core apples, slice them very thinly and mix with raisins, sugar and spices. Turn on the oven to 400°F (Gas Mark 6) and while it is heating up put the 2 oz butter in a basin to melt. Cut the pastry in half, roll and beat out as described above. It should measure *at least* 15 x 15 in when you have finished with it.

Brush the pastry with melted butter and spread with half the apple mixture, leaving a 1½ in border free from fruit. Fold in this border at the top and bottom only and roll up the pastry from right to left so that you have a filled roll, rolling as tightly as possible without breaking the pastry.

Lift carefully onto a greased baking sheet, placing the long edge underneath, and brush with melted butter. Repeat with the other half of the pastry mixture and apple mixture.

Bake in the centre of the oven for 30 to 40 minutes, until beautifully golden. Cool on the baking sheet for about 10 minutes, loosen with a palette knife and lift onto a wire rack to cool. Slice (traditionally) into diagonal pieces, cutting off the pastry edges if they tend to be bulky. Dredge with icing sugar and serve with whipped yoghurt. Apfelstrudel is also delicious served hot, but must be lifted from the baking sheet with even greater care.

This double quantity makes eight portions. If this is too much you can make half the quantity, using your spare half egg in some other cooking operation. But strudel pastry can be kept in the fridge in its floured polythene bag for up to 3 days and you might like to try some of the traditional savoury fillings, such as minced chicken or ham (or chicken *and* ham), yoghurt cheese and pineapple, minced kidney and rice, or seafood mixture. Moisten the filling with gravy or sauce. Strudel fillings should not be sloppy, but avoid dryness, which equals dullness in this context.

Pancakes

4 eggs
4 tbs milk
8 fl oz natural yoghurt
4 oz self-raising flour
½ tsp salt

Beat eggs and milk until light and fluffy. Add yoghurt gradually, beating all the time.

Mix flour and salt and add gradually to the egg mixture, beating all the time. Have a greased and hot frying pan ready and pour in enough of the mixture to make one pancake, turning it when the bottom is golden brown. Serve immediately. Serves four when filled.

PANCAKE FILLINGS

Fillings can be divided into those served warm, so that the whole pancake reaches the table piping hot, and those thoroughly chilled, so that one achieves a contrast, not only in taste but in temperature.

Yoghurt of almost any flavour can be used, either warmed or chilled. You might like to try the following:

ORANGE PANCAKES

Peel an orange very thinly so that no white pith is included. Cut the peel into matchsticks and add, with the juice, to a couple of tablespoons of clear liquid honey and a little water. Heat to boiling and keep warm.

Make the pancakes, fill with yoghurt (either chill or warm natural or orange yoghurt), fold and pour orange sauce over.

MELBA PANCAKES

Make peach sherbet as for strawberry sherbet (page 41) and freeze solid. Make a sauce by warming raspberry jam with a little water and arrowroot to thicken. Keep warm.

Make the pancakes, keeping them warm (unfolded) until you have made them all. Then quickly place a portion of sherbet on one half of each pancake, folding quickly. Pour raspberry sauce over and serve at once.

AMBROSIA PANCAKES

Chop walnuts, glacé cherries, candied peel and fold them into whipped natural yoghurt. Chill. Warm clear liquid honey with a little water.

Fill pancakes with yoghurt mixture and pour honey over.

Witchcraft Cake

Medium-sized chocolate sponge cake
1 tin stoned black cherries
2 tbs Kirsch
1 tsp cornflour
6 fl oz natural yoghurt, whipped
Chocolate curls for decoration

Strain the cherries, warm and thicken the juice with cornflour, add the cherries and allow to cool.

Split the cake lengthways and sprinkle both halves with Kirsch. Spread half the whipped yoghurt on the top of the bottom layer, place the two layers together and spoon the cherries over the top of the top layer. Decorate with the rest of the whipped yoghurt and the chocolate curls. Serves four to six.

Yoghurt Desserts

Charlotte Russe

Savoy fingers or Boudoir biscuits

CUSTARD
¼ pt milk
1½ oz sugar
Vanilla pod
1 egg
8 fl oz double cream
2 tbs sherry

FILLING
½ lb raspberries or other soft fruit
4-6 oz sugar, according to fruit used
6 fl oz hazelnut yoghurt

TO PREPARE CUSTARD
Heat the milk with sugar and the vanilla pod, which is then removed. Beat the egg, and as the milk cools add the egg drop by drop, stirring all the time. Cook very slowly, stirring all the time, until it thickens. Whip the cream with the sherry and add to cooled custard. Pour into a freezing-tray, freeze until mushy, turn into a chilled bowl, whisk and return to the freezer again until mushy.

TO PREPARE FILLING
Dissolve sugar in a minimum of water and add fruit, simmering until the liquid reduces. When cool add to yoghurt, turn into a freezing-tray and freeze until mushy.

BISCUIT CASE
Take a 7 in round cake tin and make a " collar " of tin foil or greaseproof paper, turning the top edge outwards so that the collar rests on the top edge of the tin, with the bottom edge inwards so that it forms a " step " on which the biscuits will rest. Line the sides of the tin with the biscuits so that the ends rest on the foil " step ". Spoon in first a custard layer and then a yoghurt layer, lifting the collar and biscuits if necessary. Continue layering until all the ingredients are used up. If your fillings start to defrost refreeze them, keeping the whole Charlotte in the fridge while this is being done. Remove collar when filling is complete and put the whole thing in the fridge until it is needed.

TO SERVE
Ease carefully out of the tin, place a paper frill round it and decorate.

Note: Only the tips of the biscuits should show above the filling. The care taken with the preparation of the collar is essential to prevent the biscuits from collapsing when they draw moisture from the filling. If your mixture is kept cold enough this should not happen.

Yoghurt can be frozen hard, but unlike ice cream, which has a high fat content, it goes hard and on being defrosted some whey separates out. If frozen until mushy it will hold its consistency and there will be little " run off ". Serves four.

Indian Carrot Pudding

This is a very sweet pudding and you may like to adjust the amount of sugar used. Traditionally it is served with a decorative piece of silver paper (a star perhaps) in the centre.

1 lb young carrots
½ pt milk
4 oz castor sugar
Pinch cardamom powder (which gives it a characteristic flavour)
2 oz butter
Natural yoghurt

Grate the carrots coarsely, across the grater, so that the pieces are short. Add the milk and sugar and simmer very slowly, uncovered, for 1½ hours or until all the milk has been absorbed. Stir the mixture occasionally. Add butter and cardamom and cook again until they have been absorbed.

The carrots will darken and become transparent, but should not be allowed to brown. Serve hot, with natural yoghurt, plain or whipped. Serves four.

Apple Ratafia

1 lb Bramley apples
1 tbs clear liquid honey
Packet small ratafia biscuits
2 egg whites
4 oz castor sugar
¼ pt natural yoghurt

Peel, core and slice the apples. Cook until soft in a minimum of water. Whisk egg whites until stiff and then whisk in half the sugar. Fold in the rest of the sugar and the ratafia biscuits, broken into pieces, reserving six for decoration.

Make two piles of the meringue mixture on a sheet of non-stick paper on a baking sheet, formed in rectangular piles of equal size. Bake in the coolest possible oven until crisp (about 1½ hours) but not coloured. Place, still on the paper, onto a wire rack to cool and then carefully tear off the paper.

Just before serving assemble by placing one meringue layer on a dessert dish, spreading with apple, and placing the other layer on top. Top with yoghurt whipped until it is light and fluffy. Serves four.

Melba Cocktail

4 fresh peaches
6 oz fresh raspberries
1½ oz castor sugar
3 large macaroons
4 fl oz natural yoghurt, whipped

Blanch the peaches by pouring boiling water over them and leaving them for one minute. Remove skin, stone, cut into quarters and place in the bottom of four sundae glasses. Add a layer of raspberries and leave for an hour or two so that the juices mingle. Break macaroons into pieces and place on top of the raspberries. Top with whipped yoghurt. Dredge with sugar. Serves four.

Apricot Fritters

2 lb fresh apricots

BATTER
½ lb plain flour
1 oz melted butter
1 egg
1 tbs brandy
1 dsp castor sugar
Pinch salt

MARINADE
Wineglass brandy
1 dsp castor sugar
Yoghurt topping

Dip the apricots in boiling water, peel, halve and stone. Pour over sweetened brandy and leave to soak for at least half an hour, turning frequently.

Mix the batter, without including the brandy, separating the egg and using only the yolk. Beat the mixture well until it is completely smooth and has the consistency of thin cream. Cover and let it stand in a cool place for 2 hours. Whip the egg white stiffly add to batter with brandy.

Drain the apricots (drink the brandy marinade!), dip each half in batter and drop into boiling deep fat. Remove, drain on kitchen paper.

Dredge with icing sugar and serve with whipped natural yoghurt. Serves four to six.

Apple Snow

4 Bramley apples
1 oz castor sugar
1 tsp lemon juice
2 egg whites
Natural yoghurt, whipped

Core and bake the apples in their skins until the pulp is tender and fluffy. Scoop out the pulp and press it through a sieve, adding sugar and lemon juice. Beat the egg whites until they are very stiff, fold into the apple purée and serve in individual glasses, generously topped with whipped yoghurt. Serves four.

Fruit Mélange

3 large juicy oranges
2 bananas
3 tbs shredded toasted coconut
2 dsp castor sugar
4 fl oz natural yoghurt, whipped

Dissolve the sugar in a little hot water and cool. Add the juice of one of the oranges. Peel, pith and slice the other two oranges. Peel and slice the bananas and layer the fruit in four compote or sundae dishes, pouring over the sweetened juice and topping with coconut. Top with whipped yoghurt and serve at once.

If you prefer to make this dessert in advance squeeze lemon juice over the banana, to prevent it discolouring. Serves four.

Here are some quick yoghurt desserts.

Fruit Yoghurt

Fruit yoghurt can be made with virtually any fruit, the fruit being added to the milk containers before inoculation and incubation. It is also possible to add fruit after the yoghurt has set, but in this case it is better to whip the yoghurt until it is fluffy and then fold the fruit in. This can also be done in a blender, in which case no whole pieces of fruit are left. Fruit yoghurt is usually sweetened, either with sugar or with honey.

Hazelnut and Apple Yoghurt

2 eating apples
Juice of lemon
½ oz chopped raisins
1 pt hazelnut yoghurt

Prepare hazelnut yoghurt by adding finely chopped nuts to the inoculated milk before incubation. Serves four.

Peel, core and chop apples; cover them with lemon juice at once. Add raisins and beat or blend into the yoghurt.

Tipsy Yoghurt

½ lb raisins
½ glass rum
½ pt natural yoghurt
Honey to taste

Soak the raisins in rum overnight. Blend with yoghurt sweetened with honey according to taste. Serves two to three.

Mint Yoghurt

Sweeten your inoculated milk with honey to taste. When it is ready blend with finely chopped mint leaves and a little finely chopped cucumber.

Oranges Romanesque

Choose nice-looking Jaffa oranges. Cut a small slice off the top and cut away the flesh with the point of a sharp knife so that you are left with an empty shell.

Skin the segments and blend the pulp with natural yoghurt sweetened with honey. Add a little finely shredded orange peel.

Chill the mixture until mushy, chilling the orange shells at the same time, and spoon the mixture into the shells, replacing the top slice. Chill again before serving.

Strawberry Sherbet

Take equal quantities of natural yoghurt and hulled strawberries. Freeze the yoghurt to a mush, then add the strawberries, honey and sugar to taste. Freeze until mushy again, turn into a chilled bowl and beat until smooth. Freeze again.

Note: Almost any fruit can be substituted for the strawberries. Top marks for fresh apricots!

Drinks

Yoghurt Shakes

Take equal quantities of natural yoghurt, fresh milk and fruit, sweetening to taste. Blend smooth and serve cold.

Coonardo

(the world's most refreshing drink!)
16 fl oz natural yoghurt
8 fl oz iced water
½ tsp salt
Fresh mint leaves, chopped
1 sprig mint per glass for decoration

Blend yoghurt, iced water, salt and 1 tbs chopped mint until frothy. Serve in chilled glasses. Sprinkle with a little chopped mint and place a sprig on the rim of each glass.

Yoghurt Cheese

Yoghurt cheese is more commonly known as "cottage cheese" or "crowdie". Simply place your yoghurt in a few layers of butter muslin, hang it up until the whey drips out of it and you are left with a moist curd.

The traditional place to hang the cheese bag is over the sink so that the drips don't make a mess. But the whey makes a pleasant drink in hot weather and a useful addition to soups and stews, so it is worth saving.

Once your cheese is made you can add seasoning and flavouring to it as you fancy. Salt is an obvious addition, as is freshly milled black pepper. With garlic and herbs you can parallel the expensive Boursin very closely.

Yoghurt Cheese

The dips and fillings you can make are limited only by the bounds of your culinary imagination, and we give a few here to start you on the road to the discovery of your own particular favourites.

Liptauer Cheese

4 oz yoghurt cheese
4 oz butter
3 tsp anchovy essence
1 dsp chopped capers
1 dsp chopped gherkins
1 tsp caraway seeds
1 tsp paprika
1 tsp French mustard
Pinch celery salt

Cream the butter and gradually add the other ingredients, beating well until the texture is light. This cheese keeps well, especially if packed in lidded stone jars of the type in which Stilton is sold.

Avocado Dip

2 avocado pears
8 oz yoghurt cheese
Salt
Squeeze lemon juice
Paprika

Cut avocados in half, remove the stone, scoop out the flesh and mash with lemon juice and salt. Beat in yoghurt cheese and form into a block, sprinkling liberally with paprika.

Pugaree

8 oz yoghurt cheese
1 tsp curry powder
2 tbs mango chutney
4-6 rashers streaky bacon

Cook the bacon until really crisp, drain on paper towels and crumble into fine pieces. Beat the chutney into the yoghurt cheese and add the bacon.

Crazy Maisie

8 oz yoghurt cheese
1 tsp chopped crystallized ginger
1 tsp coarsely chopped roasted peanuts
1 tbs raisins
Pinch chilli powder
Salt

Mix curry powder, salt and chilli powder well into the yoghurt cheese, then add the other ingredients.

Bargee

½ lb shelled minced mussels (or tinned clams or rock oysters)
¼ lb yoghurt cheese
2 tbs Worcester sauce

Combine mussels and cheese, then beat in Worcester sauce.

White Russian

8 oz yoghurt cheese
½ tsp finely minced onion
Jar mock caviar
Lemon wedges

Combine cheese with minced onion, then carefully fold in caviar. Top with lemon wedges.

Dipsea Dip

1 good-sized kipper
8 oz yoghurt cheese

Boil the kipper in a frying pan, then bone it and remove every particle of skin. Pound or blend smooth and beat into the yoghurt cheese.

Starters

Creamy Crab Pancakes

8 pancakes
6 oz white fish (haddock, cod etc.)
½ pt water
Bay leaf
3 oz dressed crabmeat (tinned if you can't get fresh)
½ onion
1 oz plain flour
1 oz butter or margarine
4 oz yoghurt cheese
Chopped parsley
Salt
Paprika

Poach the fish in water with the onion and bay leaf for about 10 minutes, until it is ready for flaking. Strain, reserving the stock, and flake with a fork.

Make a roux with the flour and butter and gradually add the strained fish stock. Bring to the boil, stirring all the time. Add seasoning and break 3 oz of the yoghurt cheese into small pieces, adding it piece by piece to the sauce, beating all the time. Add fish and crabmeat, adjusting seasoning if necessary.

Keeping the mixture warm make the pancakes, fill them with the mixture and roll them up. Spread them with the remaining cheese and sprinkle with chopped parsley and paprika. Serves eight.

Cheesy Apples

Choose very nice-looking apples, either very red or very green, or a few of each for a really interesting dish.

4 apples
2 oz yoghurt cheese
2 tbs milk
½ tsp vinegar
Salt, pepper and dry mustard to taste
3 oz grated Cheddar
1 stick celery, chopped
Chopped walnuts
Bowl of salt water

Mix yoghurt cheese, milk and vinegar, beat smooth, adding seasoning to taste. Add cheese, celery and walnuts.

Cut a slice from the top of each apple and drop the slices into salt water immediately to prevent them turning brown. Using a sharp knife hollow out each apple, scooping out as much flesh as possible, dropping each apple into salted water when you have finished with it.

Remove the apples from the salt water one at a time, dry them inside and out and fill with the mixture, putting the " lid " back on again. Serve with lettuce. Serves four.
Note: The same mixture can be used to fill very red large tomatoes.

Yoghurt Cheese Starters

Devilled Ham Spread

2 oz butter or margarine
2 oz yoghurt cheese
2 oz chopped ham
Few drops hot chilli sauce
Salt and pepper

Cream butter and yoghurt cheese with seasoning, then fold in ham. Spread liberally on toast triangles and serve on lettuce leaves with sliced tomato and cucumber. Serves four.

Stuffed Eggs

4 hard-boiled eggs
4 oz yoghurt cheese
2 tbs mayonnaise
Salt and pepper to taste
1 tsp chopped gherkin
Tomato wedges
Lettuce

Shell the eggs and cut them in half lengthways. Remove the yolks and mash them with yoghurt cheese and mayonnaise, beating until smooth. Add chopped gherkin and season to taste.

Pipe the mixture back into the egg whites in a decorative pattern and garnish each with a tomato wedge. Serve on lettuce. Serves four.

Note: This is again a basic recipe and the choice of additions and flavouring is a matter of personal taste. Among those recommended are pounded anchovies (or good-quality anchovy paste) or finely chopped salami.

Cream Cheese Omelette

Combine 4 oz yoghurt cheese with chopped chives and paprika. Make a 2-egg omelette, adding the cheese mixture before folding over. Serves one.

This recipe admits of many variations. Try for instance a little curry powder in the cheese, adding grated apple. Liptauer cheese (page 43) is also good.

Aztec

1 small green pepper, chopped
Knob butter
1 egg, beaten
Salt and pepper
4 oz yoghurt cheese

Cook the green pepper in the butter for 3 minutes, add the egg, salt and pepper. As it begins to set add the yoghurt cheese and cook for about a minute, stirring. Serve with green salad, on toast, or in split jacket potatoes. Serves one or two.

Shrimp Mousse

2 oz yoghurt cheese
Good pinch curry powder
Pinch chilli powder
Seasoning
Medium tin beef consommé
2 oz dressed shrimps

Mash or blend the yoghurt cheese with the curry, chilli and seasoning. Mix in half the consommé, blending well. Adjust seasoning if necessary. (It shouldn't be too highly seasoned or you won't taste the shrimps.) Pour into moistened individual moulds and refrigerate for about 30 minutes.

Unmould. Mix the shrimps with the remaining consommé, chill slightly and pour over the moulds. Refrigerate for about 10 minutes until set.

Serve chilled. A pleasant alternative to the curry and chilli would be a mixture of fresh chopped herbs. Serves two to three.

Fish

Salmon Puff

8 oz yoghurt cheese
1 tin (7 oz) red salmon
1 egg
Seasoning
8 oz puff pastry
Beaten egg to glaze

Beat the egg, drain the salmon and break it into pieces with a fork. Mix yoghurt cheese, salmon and egg and season well.

Roll out the pastry thinly and line a well-greased flan tin with it. Spoon on the mixture, cover with pastry, trim, decorate and brush with beaten egg to glaze. Bake for about 30 minutes at 400°F (Gas Mark 6).

You can of course make individual puffs, in which case the baking time will be reduced according to size. Serves four.

Salmon Loaf

This quick and easy basic recipe can be made with a variety of ingredients. (As an alternative to the salmon, try tuna fish and liver sausage.) The only requirement is that the filling should be easy to spread. The loaf needs no cooking.

Medium tin salmon, drained
8 oz yoghurt cheese
4 oz butter or margarine
18 cream crackers
Paprika
Lettuce and cucumber and tomato slices for garnish

Mix yoghurt cheese and butter. Drain, mash and season the salmon. Lay two cream crackers side by side on a dish and spread them with the butter/cheese mixture. Top with two more biscuits and spread these with salmon. Alternate biscuits spread with butter/cheese and biscuits spread with salmon, until biscuits and salmon are used up.

Cover the top and sides with the remaining butter/cheese mixture, piping lines along the edges and decorating in any other way that takes your fancy. Arrange lettuce leaves, and cucumber and tomato slices around. Serves four.

Haddock Quiche

½ lb shortcrust pastry
½ lb smoked haddock
1 oz butter
2 oz button mushrooms
2 eggs
2 tbs milk
4 oz yoghurt cheese
Juice of 1 lemon
Salt and freshly milled black pepper
Parsley to garnish

Prepare an 8 in flan tin, line it with pastry and bake blind.

Cook the haddock in a little water. Slice the mushrooms finely and fry for a few minutes in butter. Beat the eggs, milk, yoghurt cheese and lemon juice together and season well. Line the flan tin with the fish and mushrooms and pour the beaten egg mixture over. Bake until set and golden brown. Garnish with parsley. Serve either hot or cold. Serves four.

Desserts

The Great Cheesecake Controversy

Every cheesecake-maker is convinced that he/she has the only possible cheesecake recipe in the world. In fact there are a large number of good recipes going the rounds. Here we quote just a few of them.

BISCUIT CRUST
12 digestive biscuits
Pinch cinnamon
3 oz castor sugar
4 oz melted butter

Crush biscuits to a powder and mix with cinnamon, sugar and melted butter. Press well into a greased round tin.

Note: This crust is best left unbaked and is very suitable for use with an uncooked filling.

PASTRY CRUST
3 oz butter
1 egg, beaten
6 oz plain flour
1 tsp sugar

Cream butter and beaten egg. Add sifted flour and sugar. Roll out thinly and line a greased round tin.

FILLING 1
8 oz yoghurt cheese
4 oz castor sugar
½ pt double cream
3 eggs, separated
2 oz flour
Grated rind and juice of 1 lemon

Whip the yoghurt cheese to a thin cream, preferably in a blender. Add sugar and cream and whip again until absolutely smooth.

Beat the egg yolks and one white together, adding flour, grated lemon rind and juice. Add to the mixture, beating smooth. Beat the remaining whites very stiff and fold gently into the mixture.

Spoon into a tin lined with the pastry case and bake in a slow oven (250°F, Gas Mark 2) for an hour. Leave in while the oven cools. When cold chill in the refrigerator.

FILLING 2
2 oz butter
3 oz castor sugar
1½ oz freshly ground almonds
1 oz semolina
8 oz yoghurt cheese
Grated rind and juice of 1 lemon
2 oz sultanas
3 egg whites

Cream butter and sugar. Add all the other ingredients, except egg whites, stirring until smooth. Whip the egg whites very stiff and fold in gently. Pour into pastry-lined flan tin.

Bake in the centre of the oven at 350°F (Gas Mark 4) until the filling is set, about 45 minutes, then reduce heat to prevent the top browning, for about another 10 minutes.

FILLING 3 (Uncooked)
6 oz yoghurt cheese
Juice and grated peel of 1 lemon
Small tin condensed milk

Beat yoghurt cheese with lemon juice and grated peel until very smooth. Fold in condensed milk.
This filling is best used with an uncooked biscuit crust.

ORANGE CHEESECAKE
Substitute orange juice and grated orange peel for lemon.

RUM AND RAISIN CHEESECAKE
Soak raisins overnight in rum and fold carefully into cheesecake mixture.

CHERRY CHEESECAKE
Drain the juice from a can of dark cherries and reserve it. Fold cherries into cheesecake mixture. Make a stiff jelly from the juice, adding dark red colouring. As it begins to set pour it over the top of the chilled cheesecake.

Heart of Cream
(Coeur à la crême)

Traditionally this should be made in a heart-shaped mould or cake tin, or better still in individual heart-shaped Coeur à la Crême moulds.

8 oz yoghurt cheese
2 tbs icing sugar
½ pt double cream
½ lb strawberries
Lemon juice
Castor sugar

Blend yoghurt cheese and icing sugar in a blender until absolutely smooth, or pass it through a nylon sieve. Add the cream and whisk the mixture until it is smooth and soft. Press the mixture firmly into a mould or several small moulds. Refrigerate overnight.

Drain any " run-off " from the moulds and turn out on to dessert plates. If it still looks a little moist blot it very carefully with tissues. Surround with hulled sliced strawberries sprinkled with lemon juice and castor sugar. Serves four.

 *Honey*

Honey

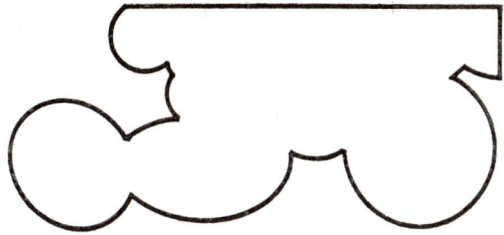

ALTHOUGH yoghurt could possibly be considered, at least to Westerners, an acquired taste, almost everybody in the world likes honey. Honey is good to eat, is one of the few virtually totally non-allergic foods and is easily assimilated by the body. Rich in levelose and dextrose, it acts as an almost instant energizer. It provides a generous supply of vitamins B1 and C, riboflavin, penthothenic acid, pyridoxine and niacin.

But it contains something more, something that might be called its own "X factor". It is impossible to manufacture synthetic honey. Its exact composition is known. It is apparently capable of analysis. But when scientists try to put it together what they get is not honey. Palatable, yes, pleasant, yes, nutritious, yes. But this synthetic substance, even when loaded with vitamins and minerals, does not confer the special health benefits imparted by natural honey. Something in the processing of the honey by the bee defies analysis, but is essential if we are to obtain maximum health benefit.

Both specific and general claims can be made regarding the healthful effects of honey. From studies of groups of children fed on a variety of food additives it can be shown that the honey eaters improve in general health, blood count, weight, height and energy.

Honey is a specific against sleeplessness (try it in hot milk before going to bed), a better relaxant than a tranquillizing pill, a safe long-term laxative and a gentle internal disinfectant, effective even in cases of such severe conditions as dysentery, typhoid and peritonitis. It is also thought by some to be anti-haemorraghic, aiding the clotting of the blood. Many people find that it promotes bodily warmth, and if you eat honey regularly in one form or other you will usually need less of other foods, thus avoiding the complications of too rich or too heavy a diet. Honey can cause weight reduction in some people who have a faulty metabolism where fat is concerned, as the quick absorption of honey causes fat to "burn up" rapidly and completely. The list of cures effected by the eating of honey is almost endless. Credence may be given to them because bees are capable of manufacturing at least six antibiotics essential to the making of honey and the honeycomb.

These claims may seem extravagant, but the test is to take honey yourself when you feel unwell. If you confine yourself to honey and water for a few days (providing your condition warrants abstention from other foods) you are very likely to derive a great deal of benefit from it. Certainly honey will help you to ward off a cold, and there is no better relief from a tickly cough than a sip of honey and lemon mixed with a little glycerine. Honey and apple cider vinegar (oxymel) have helped many a sufferer from arthritis; the chewing of " cappings " from a honeycomb will also clear a stuffy nose instantly.

Honeys vary a great deal in taste according to their region of origin, the variation depending not only on the flowers from which the nectar is gathered, but on such factors as rainfall and the mineral content of the soil. One can become as much an expert in honey taste as in wines, and most of us have our favourites for which we usually have to pay a higher price than for honey of no specific variety. The most readily obtainable British honeys include clover and heather (you can also occasionally buy box honey which is made from the small white flowers of the box hedges). Rose or lavender honeys are considered specialities and carry the scent and flavour of the flowers from which the nectar is gathered. Honeys carry the designation " heather ", " lavender " and so on when the predominating flavour is that of a particular flower; but this doesn't mean to say that no other nectar is used, since one cannot monitor the work of every individual bee! But it appears that bees are not guided merely by the availability of any particular type of flower and will actually seek out their own particular " tribal flower ".

Orange blossom honey usually comes from California and is often sold with a piece of honeycomb inside the jar. Australian honey almost always carries a tang of eucalyptus from the gum tree flowers. It has a stronger taste than many other honeys, especially the mild Mexican honey, but many people like it very much indeed.

Honey keeps almost indefinitely. A jar of it found not so long ago in an Egyptian tomb is estimated to be 3,300 years old. Its condition is perfect. Honey is best kept in stone or glass jars, as it will eventually corrode the sides of metal containers. It improves with keeping, just as wine does, the aroma increasing during storage. Sometimes the nectar of certain flowers (notably those of the Spanish chestnut) gives an unpleasant odour to the resulting honey, but this disappears after it has been stored for a year or two.

Honey can be used as a substitute for sugar in cooking, for although heating naturally destroys most of the vitamins other health-giving properties remain, including, it seems, the mysterious " X factor ".

Dressings

Honey Dressing

4 tbs clear liquid honey
8 oz olive oil
¼ pt wine vinegar

Place all ingredients in a blender and blend for 1 minute.

Honey Mayonnaise

2 eggs
2 tbs clear liquid honey
1 tsp made mustard
Salt and cayenne pepper to taste
½ pt olive oil
1 tsp tarragon vinegar
Juice of 2 lemons

Break the eggs into a basin, making sure that only the yolks slide in and the whites remain behind in the shell. Add honey, mustard, salt and cayenne pepper. Stir with a wooden spoon to mix. Beat in the oil drop by drop, always beating the same way (don't change hands even if your arm feels as if it were going to drop off), until the mixture takes on the consistency of batter. If it curdles, and won't improve with beating, beat another egg yolk in another basin and add it to the mayonnaise gradually, beating all the time.

When the mayonnaise is quite stiff add the vinegar and lemon juice, stirring it in.

Mayonnaise Aspic

A decorative alternative to a plain salad is a mayonnaise mould made with aspic jelly. This can take the form of a jelly made in a ring mould and served with salad in the centre, or of salad ingredients actually incorporated into the mould. In the latter case lettuce, chicory or other green salad leaves should not be added to the mould because they would wilt, but chopped celery, cucumber, radishes or cooked peas take on added taste and attractiveness when served in this fashion.

Another alternative: chopped meat or poultry or flakes of cooked fish can be incorporated into the mould and served surrounded with salad.

To make mayonnaise aspic take:

½ pt aspic jelly
3 tbs mayonnaise

Make the jelly and cool it. While it is still liquid mix in the mayonnaise and stir until it begins to thicken. Pour into a wetted mould.

When adding salad ingredients, layer these inside the mould and pour on the aspic just as it is beginning to set. Chill.

Vinaigrette

6 tbs olive oil
2 tbs tarragon vinegar
2 tsp honey
½ tsp chopped capers
½ tsp chopped onion
Good pinch basil, fennel, dill
½ tsp chopped mint

Combine all ingredients and stir well. Stir again before serving.

Starters

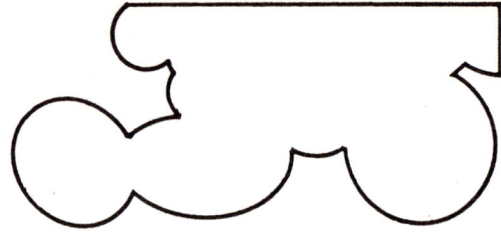

Pears Vinaigrette

2 ripe dessert pears
Vinaigrette dressing
Lettuce
Freshly milled black pepper

Peel, core and halve the pears lengthways. Arrange each half on a lettuce leaf, pour over the vinaigrette dressing and sprinkle with black pepper. Serves four.

Sherried Grapefruit

2 grapefruit
Glass sweet sherry
4 tsp clear liquid honey
1 oz butter

Halve the grapefruit, cut out the centre core and loosen the segments with a sharp knife. Pour sherry and honey into the centre of each half and top with a knob of butter.

Bake in a hot oven (400°F, Gas Mark 6) for about 15 minutes. Pour over any juice that has run out and serve hot. Serves four.

Lemon Crab

1 small tin crabmeat
1 punnet cress
3 hard-boiled eggs
Freshly milled black pepper
1 tsp lemon juice
Grated peel of 1 lemon
¼ pt mayonnaise

Cut, wash and drain the cress, sprinkling a little at the bottom of four sundae glasses. Drain the crabmeat and chop it coarsely. Shell and chop the eggs and mix lightly with the crabmeat. Season with black pepper.

Add lemon juice and grated peel to mayonnaise, then add to eggs and crabmeat, mixing well. Pile mixture into glasses and sprinkle remaining cress round the edge. Serves four.

Kipper Cole Slaw

½ small white cabbage
6 fl oz natural yoghurt
3 tbs mayonnaise
8 oz kipper fillets
Freshly milled black pepper
Tomato slices for garnish

MARINADE
4 fl oz white wine
2 tbs olive oil

Marinate the kipper fillets overnight. Shred cabbage finely and coat with a Cole Slaw Dressing (see recipe below), sprinkling with black pepper. Drain and skin kipper fillets, roll up into strips and arrange on top of the cabbage. Garnish with tomato slices and serve with lettuce. Serves two or three.

Cole Slaw Dressing

½ pt natural yoghurt
3 tbs clear liquid honey
Juice of one lemon

Whip yoghurt until it is fluffy. Add honey and lemon juice and whip again. Serve with Cole Slaw salad.

Meat

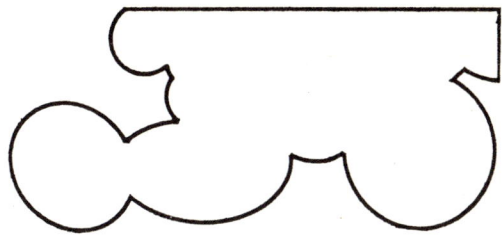

Honey Duck

1 duck, trussed and drawn

STUFFING
*1 lb pork sausagemeat
2 oz fresh breadcrumbs
Grated peel of 1 orange
½ tsp mixed herbs
Seasoning*

GLAZE
*1 tbs clear liquid honey
Juice of 1 orange*

GRAVY
*Giblets
½ pt stock
Flour
Seasoning*

GARNISH
*Orange slices
Watercress*

Mix ingredients for stuffing and pack into duck, sewing or skewering down the loose skin so that it doesn't come out during cooking.

Place the duck in a roasting tin and prick the skin all over with a large needle to allow the fat to escape. Rub the skin with salt and roast in a fairly hot oven (Gas Mark 6, 400°F) for half an hour, then reduce the heat to 350° (Gas Mark 4), and cook for another 1½ hrs until nearly done. Glaze with honey and orange juice and return to the oven for not more than 15 minutes.

Prepare stock by simmering the giblets in ½ pt water. Strain. When the duck is cooked take the drippings from the roasting tin, make a roux with a little flour and stir in the stock. Bring to the boil and simmer until thickened. Adjust seasoning.

Garnish with watercress and orange slices. Serves six.

Honey Glazed Bacon

*Boned forehock of bacon, 3 to 4 lb in weight
Bay leaf
Blade mace
Peppercorns
Few cloves*

GLAZE
*3 tbs clear liquid honey
Juice of 1 orange (or pineapple juice)*

GRAVY
*½ pt bacon stock
1 level tbs cornflour*

Roll and tie bacon joint and cover with water in a large casserole, adding bay, mace, peppercorns and cloves. Bring to the boil and simmer for 50 minutes. Drain, reserving ½ pt strained stock for gravy.

Prepare the glaze by mixing honey and orange juice. Score the bacon rind by cutting in a diamond pattern, place it in a roasting tin and pour the glaze over slowly so that it soaks into the incisions in the rind. Roast in a moderate oven for up to an hour (until tender), basting occasionally. Remove string before serving and pour pan drippings over the joint.

Make gravy from stock and cornflour, seasoning well. You can also make your gravy from the pan drippings, but it will be rather sweet. Serves six.

Colonial Goose

This is a New Zealand recipe and is said to have originated when the early settlers grew tired of eternally eating plain roast lamb. The recipe calls for a leg of lamb, but you can equally well use shoulder or even breast—or even mutton.

1 leg of lamb, boned

STUFFING
1 tbs dried apricots, chopped
4 oz fresh breadcrumbs
2 oz butter or margarine
1 tbs clear liquid honey
1 grated onion
1 tsp mixed herbs
1 egg
Seasoning

MARINADE
2 glasses red wine
1 glass wine vinegar
1 tbs clear liquid honey
Bay leaf
6 peppercorns
Clove garlic, crushed

Place chopped apricots and breadcrumbs in a bowl. Melt butter and honey in a saucepan and add, with the grated onion and herbs, to the breadcrumbs and apricots. Beat the egg and use it to bind the other ingredients. Season.

Trim excess fat from the boned meat and spoon the stuffing into the cavity left by the removal of the bone. Sew the edges of the cavity together, using fine twine or dental floss. Make sure the stuffing is packed well inside.

Mix marinade ingredients and marinate the joint for about 6 hours, turning the meat occasionally and basting with the marinade.

Roast at 350°F (Gas Mark 4) for approximately 20 minutes for each pound of meat, covering with foil if the skin starts to burn. Remove string before serving. Serves four to six, according to the size of the joint.

Chicken Celeste

4 chicken pieces
Salt and pepper
Few rashers fat bacon
3 tbs clear liquid honey
2 level tbs French mustard
1 tsp curry powder (or to taste)
1 crushed clove garlic

Skin the chicken pieces, lay them in a fire-proof dish, sprinkle with salt and pepper and cover with bacon rashers. Mix other ingredients and pour over. Bake in a moderate oven for about an hour until pieces are tender, turning them over at half time and basting occasionally.

Serve with plain gravy *and* a sauce made from the pan drippings, though this may be a little sweet for some tastes. Serves four.

Baked Gammon with Orange Honey Glaze

Buy a neat round gammon joint and cut it across in slices at least 1 in thick. Alternatively, if you know a delicatessen where they slice their own ham, cajole them into cutting you four 1 in slices.

GLAZE
1 tin frozen concentrated orange juice
4 tbs clear liquid honey

Take a large baking tray (at least 13 x 9 in and 2 in deep) and place the gammon slices in it.

Dilute the orange concentrate to make 1 pint of liquid and pour it over the slices. Bake at 350°F (Gas Mark 4) for 1 hour. Remove the tray from the oven and brush the slices with honey. Return the tray to the oven for 10 minutes to set the glaze. Serves four.

Main-Course Salads

Salad Niçoise

6 small potatoes
4 oz whole green beans
1 lettuce
Vinaigrette
1 tin tuna fish or salmon
1 tin anchovy fillets
2 hard-boiled eggs, quartered
1 onion, sliced
4 tomatoes, quartered
12 black olives, pitted
1 green pepper, thinly sliced

Boil the potatoes in their jackets until just tender; peel and slice. Cook beans, leaving them whole, and drain. Put the potatoes and beans in the refrigerator to chill. Wash the lettuce and shake well to dry. Separate the leaves and line a large bowl with them. Sprinkle with vinaigrette dressing, also sprinkling the potatoes and beans. Drain the fish and separate into chunks.

Layer all ingredients on top of the lettuce. The enjoyment of this salad (and indeed any salad) can be considerably heightened by the artistic arrangement of the ingredients, and you have a good assortment of colours and textures to make it attractive. Save the olives, egg quarters and tomato quarters for the top. Sprinkle again with vinaigrette and chill before serving. Serves four.

Tuna Salad

1 tin tuna fish
1 tin butter beans, drained
4 spring onions, finely chopped (or 6 chives if in season)
3 tbs vinaigrette
Salt and freshly milled black pepper

Divide the tuna fish into chunks with a fork. Add to beans and onions or chives and mix well. Moisten with vinaigrette dressing and season. Serve with lettuce and any other salad ingredients you fancy. Serves four.

Salad Capri

6 oz long-grain rice
1 green pepper
4 large tomatoes
1 pt prawns
1 small tin whole-kernel sweet corn
Vinaigrette
Salt and freshly milled black pepper

Boil the rice, drain, rinse and cool. Remove seeds and core from the pepper, cover with water, bring to the boil, simmer for 5 minutes, drain, cool and cut into strips. Cover the tomatoes with boiling water, leave for a minute, drain, skin and cut into slices. Shell prawns, drain sweet corn.

Saving a few prawns for garnish, mix all ingredients with vinaigrette. Season. Pile on a serving dish and garnish with remaining prawns. Serves four.

Or make a bed of rice on a rectangular dish and layer the ingredients in "stripes", sprinkling liberally with dressing.

Dandelion Salad

Don't despise the humble dandelion as a salad ingredient. When young and fresh the leaves are very reminiscent of the expensive endive, which can be substituted if you are not resident in dandelion country!

½ lb dandelion leaves
4 oz streaky bacon
2 eggs
3 oz Gruyère cheese
1 clove garlic, crushed
Vinaigrette
Salt and freshly milled black pepper

Cut the rind from the bacon, chop it finely and fry until the fat runs out. Drain and cool. Hard boil the eggs, cool, shell and chop. Dice the cheese. Wash the dandelion leaves well.

Mix all ingredients and coat well with vinaigrette. Season lightly and serve immediately. Serves four.

Flower Garden Salad

If you have a garden and believe that salads should be pretty, try this unusual and attractive one.

4 marigold heads
Few nasturtium heads and seeds
Lettuce
Chopped chives or spring onions
4 tomatoes, quartered
4 hard-boiled eggs, quartered
Vinaigrette

Wash the lettuce, separate the leaves, tear them into pieces and cover with vinaigrette dressing. Place a layer in a large bowl and add eggs, tomatoes and chives or spring onions. Place remaining lettuce on top and scatter marigold petals and nasturtium flowers and seeds on top. Serves four.

Looks good enough to eat doesn't it?

Side Salads

ORANGE AND WATERCRESS SALAD

Peel oranges and remove the pith. Slice across thinly with a sharp knife and lay the slices on a long dish, overlapping them slightly. Garnish lavishly with carefully washed and trimmed watercress and sprinkle liberally with a dressing of lemon juice and honey.

Note: Vinegar should never be used with watercress, as it makes it quite indigestible for some people.

CUCUMBER SALAD

Chill a cucumber, score along its length with a fork and cut into slices. Serve with vinaigrette dressing and sprinkle with finely chopped chives and fresh dill, or a sprinkling of dill seed.

PINEAPPLE SALAD

Shred half a white cabbage. Core, peel and chop a cooking apple. Dice a stick of celery. Mix all together and add a drained tin of pineapple chunks (or, infinitely preferable, use fresh pineapple). Coat with mayonnaise.

Serve on lettuce leaves, garnishing with a few halved pineapple chunks or fresh pineapple slivers.

TOMATO AND BASIL SALAD

Slice tomatoes thinly with a very sharp knife and lay the slices on a long dish, overlapping them slightly. Sprinkle with basil (fresh if possible, in which case it should be finely chopped) and with freshly milled black pepper. Cover with vinegar.

POTATO SALAD

Boil potatoes in their jackets until just cooked; peel and dice. Finely chop an onion, add to diced potatoes and coat with mayonnaise to which salt has been added. Garnish with chopped parsley and paprika.

Desserts

Baked Apples

Medium-sized cooking apples
1 dsp clear liquid honey
Chopped dates
Small knob butter or margarine for each apple

Wash, dry and core the apples. Make a cut in the skin round the circumference with a sharp knife. Stand the apples in a greased baking tin, and fill the centres with a mixture of chopped dates and honey, topping with a small piece of butter. Bake for about ½ hour at 400°F (Gas Mark 6) until the apple pulp is soft.

Note: Raisins or chopped ginger can be used as an alternative to dates.

Malvern Pudding

Local history claims that this pudding was invented by a doctor who considered pastry too indigestible for his patients. It is a very pleasant summer pudding, economical and easy to prepare.

½ loaf stale white bread
1 lb dark soft fruit (blackberries, blackcurrants, bilberries etc.)
4 oz clear liquid honey

Stew the fruit with the honey, adding plenty of water to make juice. Line the bottom and sides of a smallish ungreased pudding basin with bread slices, packing the bread down tightly. Pour in fruit and juice and top with bread slices. Place a plate on top of the basin, and place a weight on top (traditionally a flat iron) and leave it to stand in a cool place overnight. The weight on top of the expanding bread should pack it sufficiently for it to be turned out next day, and served as you would serve a pudding with a pastry crust. Serves four.

Serve with yoghurt or cream.

Note: Dark fruit is specified because it gives the pudding an attractive look. Pallid fruits make a pallid pudding. The exception to the soft-fruit rule is damsons, a rather neglected fruit deserving of renewed attention.

Bara Mwyar

Closely allied to Malvern pudding, gastronomically and geographically, is Welsh blackberry pudding. It is a traditional easy "hurry-up" country recipe, because blackberry time was also harvest time, when farmers' wives were busy even if the children had time for blackberrying.

Simply put blackberries in a saucepan with just enough water to cover and simmer, throwing in small torn-off pieces of bread to absorb the juice, until the consistency is the way you like it, possibly a bit moist. Sweeten with honey and serve hot or cold with cream or whipped yoghurt.

It is delicious slightly chilled.

Battered Bananas

4 bananas
3 oz plain flour
1 egg, beaten
Pinch salt
Water to mix

SYRUP
6 tbs clear liquid honey
Water

Prepare the batter with flour, egg, salt and enough water to give it a good coating consistency. Peel the bananas and halve lengthways. Prepare honey syrup by warming the honey and water and keeping it warm.

Dip each piece of banana in batter and fry in deep hot oil until golden, draining well on kitchen paper. Pour syrup over. Serve with whipped yoghurt. Serves four.

A more elaborate version of this recipe is rather spectacular: instead of preparing honey syrup make a glaze with 6 tbs sugar and 3 tbs water, boiling until it becomes straw-coloured. Plunge the base of the saucepan into cold water to stop it cooking further. When the batter-coated bananas have been fried, dip each fritter into the syrup and drop it immediately into a bowl of iced water, when the surface will crystallize. Honey toffee can be used instead of sugar syrup.

Butterscotch Sundae

Brick vanilla ice cream
3 bananas
4 oz chopped walnuts
¼ lb honey butterscotch (see page 65)

Place alternate layers of ice cream, sliced bananas and chopped walnuts into sundae cups or glasses, finishing with ice cream. Chill. Just before serving top with butterscotch broken very fine with a toffee hammer, or crushed between two layers of greaseproof paper with a rolling pin. Serves four.

Baked Honey Custard

3 eggs
1¼ pt milk
4 tbs clear liquid honey
½ tsp vanilla essence
Pinch salt

Beat the eggs slightly, until just mixed, and stir in other ingredients. Pour into a greased fire-proof dish, or individual fire-proof cups, standing them in a pan with a little water in it. Bake in a medium oven until the custard sets but is still soft (about ¾ hour for a large dish, ½ hour for small cups.)

Serve hot or cold with stewed fruit. Serves three to four.

Peaches Royale

3 fresh peaches
1 tbs clear liquid honey
1 tbs Cointreau
1 tbs orange juice
Savoy or Boudoir biscuits
Natural yoghurt

Skin and halve the peaches and remove the stones. Mix Cointreau, honey and orange juice and pour over peaches. Chill thoroughly. Serve with Savoy or Boudoir biscuits and thin or whipped natural yoghurt. Serves three to six, according to your generosity where the peaches are concerned.

Note: Tinned peaches can be used.

Bread and Cakes

Honey Fruit Bread

8 oz butter
8 oz soft brown sugar
4 eggs
1 lb self-raising flour
1 level tsp mixed spice
1 level tsp ginger
4 bananas, mashed
4 tbs clear liquid honey
4 oz chopped dates
4 oz chopped glacé cherries
4 oz sultanas
4 oz raisins
4 oz chopped walnuts

Cream butter and sugar and beat in eggs. Fold flour mixed with spice and ginger into the creamed butter and sugar mixture, alternating with the mashed bananas and honey; then stir in fruit and nuts.

Spoon into a large well-greased loaf tin. Bake at 350°F (Gas Mark 4) for about 1 hour, checking for signs of scorching on top and covering with greaseproof paper if necessary.

Turn out on to a wire rack to cool and brush the top with warmed honey. Leave for a day or two before slicing. Serve plain or buttered.

Flat Bread

2 oz butter or margarine
8 oz wholemeal flour
8 fl oz natural yoghurt
1 tbs clear liquid honey
1 tsp salt

Rub butter into flour, add yoghurt, honey and salt and knead vigorously. Roll small pieces of dough into small balls, then beat each ball very thin and flat with your fist or a rolling pin.

Drop each piece into very hot cooking fat and it will puff up and become very like a poppadum. Serve with curry.

Flat bread can also be cooked on a very hot greased griddle, and can be eaten spread with yoghurt cheese or with dips.

Honey Ginger Cake

4 oz butter or margarine
2 oz soft brown sugar
5 oz clear liquid honey
2 eggs, well beaten
1 tsp lemon juice
8 oz self-raising flour
Pinch salt
1 tsp ground ginger
Glacé icing
2 oz preserved ginger

Cream the butter, add the sugar and cream again. Beat in the honey gradually and then gradually add the well-beaten eggs and lemon juice. Sieve flour, salt and ground ginger and fold into creamed mixture.

Pour the mixture into a greased tin and cover with a piece of greaseproof paper. Bake in a moderate oven (350°F, Gas Mark 4) for about 1 hour.

Turn out carefully onto a wire rack. Ice with glacé icing when cold, decorating with chopped preserved ginger.

Petits-fours

These tiny "bite-size" cakes are a traditional accompaniment to after-dinner coffee. A really grand petit-four is made simply with marzipan (see page 66), iced and decorated, but nowadays marzipan on its own is considered a little rich, so petits-fours are usually made with a sponge-cake base and a thin marzipan layer on top. They often appear, incorrectly, at the tea table. This we think rather a pity, especially as few people would eat more than one or two after a good dinner; their original purpose was to serve as a gesture of courtesy to those who didn't take liqueurs or brandy with their coffee, as it was considered impolite and parsimonious to offer coffee on its own.

Be this as it may, petits-fours made with really good marzipan (seldom met with these days unless you make your own) are delicious and pretty conceits. But in an effort to keep up with the times we have given instructions for their manufacture *with* sponge cake underneath the marzipan.

Sponge cake
Honey marzipan (page 66)
Apricot jam
Glacé icing in various flavours and colours
Crystallized fruit or flowers

If you can get it buy "sheet sponge", which is a thin sponge layer very suitable for making petits-fours. If this is not available and you don't feel like making your own, buy sponge flan cases. When you cut them into the traditional diamond shapes the left-over pieces can be trimmed into attractive crescent shapes. This shaping is best done after the marzipan is in place.

Roll out the marzipan thinly. Warm the apricot jam, brush it over the sponge and top with marzipan firmly pressed down. Cut into the required shapes.

Make glacé icing in various colours, including chocolate (traditional!) and ice the cakes over the top and down the sides. Decorate each cake with an almond stuck in at an angle, a glacé cherry, a piece of angelica or sliver of crystallized fruit.

If you have a fancy to garnish your petits-fours with real crystallized flowers, these are easy to make, but difficult to buy. Suitable for crystallizing are primroses, violets, jasmine and other soft-petalled flowers, rose petals and mimosa balls. Wash the flowers or petals free from dust in cold water and cut off stems. Make a syrup with ½ lb granulated sugar to a pint of water. While it is boiling drop in the flowers or petals, removing them immediately with a straining spoon and laying them on greaseproof paper to dry. When they are quite dry (which will probably be next day) boil up the same syrup and dip as before. Continue until the flowers are completely crystallized. The same syrup is used because it is essential that it should become slightly stronger each time; this is achieved by the repeated boiling up.

Chocolate Honey Cookies

2 tsp clear liquid honey
8 oz butter or margarine
6 tbs chocolate spread
½ lb semi-sweet biscuits, crushed
4 oz icing sugar (for glacé icing)

Place honey, butter and chocolate spread in a saucepan and heat until it melts, stirring all the time. Add crushed biscuits, mixing well in, until smooth.
 Pour the mixture into a greased shallow tin and leave to set. When cool cut into bars or shapes and decorate with glacé icing as desired.

Note: This is such an easy recipe that it is very suitable for children to try, especially as there is very little heat required and no danger of anything boiling over.

Mockeroons

These biscuits contain almond essence and taste very much like macaroons, though the texture is coarser. If you omit the almond essence and add vanilla essence they will emerge as flapjacks.

3 oz butter or margarine
1 tbs demerara sugar
1½ tbs clear liquid honey
Few drops almond essence
4 oz self-raising flour
Pinch salt
½ lb rolled oats

Beat butter, sugar, honey and essence until the mixture is smooth and creamy. Work in dry ingredients and form the mixture into a roll. Cut the roll across into 24 slices, shape each slice into a ball and flatten it between the palms of your hands. Place on a greased baking tray. Bake in a moderate oven for 15-20 minutes.

Fairings
(Gingerbread Men)

Among the long past and almost forgotten traditions of country life are the gingerbread figures one used to be able to buy at fairs. They are easy enough to be made by children, who can be kept amused for hours constructing the dough into various shapes, are among the best sellers at charity fêtes and, formed into Father Christmas figures and iced accordingly, look good on any Christmas tree.

4 oz butter or margarine
1 lb plain flour
2 oz brown sugar
½ oz ground ginger
½ tsp ground cinnamon
2 tbs clear liquid honey

Cream the butter and add dry ingredients, then warmed honey. Knead into a thick smooth paste, adding a little more honey if necessary to keep the dough from cracking. Roll out thinly and cut into human or animal shapes. Place on a greased baking sheet and bake in a moderate oven for about 15 minutes, taking care not to let them scorch.
 Decoration, by tradition, entailed currants for eyes and waistcoat buttons, but these tend to harden during baking and it is better to add such embellishments in icing after the figures have cooled.

Sweets

Basic Honey Fudge

¼ pt single cream or "top of the milk"
Small tin sweetened condensed milk
4 oz butter or margarine
2 tbs clear liquid honey
1 lb icing sugar
Pinch cream of tartar

Mix all ingredients in a heavy-bottomed saucepan. Bring to the boil slowly, stirring all the time and making sure that all ingredients dissolve evenly. Boil rapidly, stirring occasionally, for about 8 minutes, until a small amount dropped into a little water forms a soft ball (240°F, if you have a sugar thermometer).

Remove the pan from the heat, cool slightly and then beat mixture until thick. Pour into a greased shallow tin about 7 in square. Leave until almost set and mark deeply into small squares. When quite set remove from tin, break into pieces and place on a wire rack to harden.

Coffee Fudge

Take 1 tbs strong coffee, or ½ tsp instant coffee dissolved in ½ tbs of hot water, and add just before beating up the mixture.

Chocolate Fudge

Melt ½ oz bitter chocolate over hot water and add just before beating up.

Ginger Fudge

Add 1 tsp powdered ginger to the original ingredients, then finely chopped preserved ginger just before beating up the mixture.

Cherry Walnut Fudge

Chop 2 oz glacé cherries, 2 oz walnuts, and add with 1 tsp vanilla essence just before beating.

Rum and Raisin Fudge

Soak 1 tbs raisins in rum overnight. Add just before beating.

Honey Popcorn

The making (and eating) of popcorn is a pleasant pursuit on a rainy day during the school holidays. If you haven't got a proper popper, corn can be popped in any heavy pan with a tightly fitting lid. Don't ever try to pop corn in an unlidded pan, because it has an incredibly wide firing range and tends to land on the top of cupboards and in milk jugs! The principle is simple . . . if you subject the corn to sufficient dry heat, the kernels will puff up and burst. Always use the correct "popping" corn. On the other hand you can use the simple short cut of substituting puffed wheat, puffed rice or other puffed cereal.

Take 1 lb clear liquid honey and boil it until it is very thick. Remove it from the heat and add the popped corn or cereal. When it is cool enough to handle form it into balls, or any other shape you fancy.

Popcorn balls tied with ribbon make excellent decorations for children's parties and for the Christmas tree.

Honey Butterscotch

1 lb clear liquid honey
¼ lb butter
½ tsp salt
Vanilla essence

Boil the honey, stirring all the time, until it thickens and a tiny quantity dropped in water will harden instantly. Remove from heat and stir in melted butter, salt and vanilla essence.

Pour into a well-greased shallow tin and mark into small squares when almost set. Break up into squares when cold and (unless for immediate consumption) wrap in greaseproof paper because butterscotch becomes very sticky if exposed to the air.

Honey Humbugs

You are better off with a marble slab when making humbugs, and if you intend to become a devoted sweetmaker fix a hook a couple of feet above the slab, on which to pull the toffee. Although they are quite easy to make nobody seems to bother with humbugs these days, which is a pity because in addition to tasting delicious they have an easily achieved air of professionalism about them.

Make honey toffee as follows:
¾ lb demerara sugar
2 oz butter
2 tbs " top of the milk "
2 tbs clear liquid honey
Vanilla or peppermint essence
Colouring as required

Boil sugar, butter and milk, stirring until the sugar dissolves. Add honey and continue boiling until a small quantity dropped in water hardens immediately. Remove from heat and stir in flavouring and colouring.

Pour a generous quantity of cooking oil on to the marble slab and oil your hands well. Pour the toffee on to the slab and as soon as it is cool enough start to maul it about a bit. Pull out lumps of it as if you were pulling bubble gum, throwing it over the hook, if you have one, to pull it out.

After a while the toffee will become silvery and cloudy, and when the whole mass is of equal consistency and colouring form it into a long roll about ½ in in diameter. Dip the blades of your kitchen scissors in cooking oil and make a cut from side to side, and the next from front to back and—you have a humbug!

Space the humbugs out on greaseproof paper, making sure that they don't touch. When they are completely cold wipe them clean of oil with tissues.

The making of humbugs is one of the most fascinating processes in cookery and a great deal of variation can be introduced in flavouring and colouring. Children love enormous cheek-swelling humbugs, which are of course quicker to make than the smaller ones. But this is not a recipe for small children to try because they almost invariably burn themselves with hot toffee. Safety lies in moving quickly. Slow workers get scorched!

As expertise develops you can create two-toned humbugs (very professional) by making two batches of different colour. Once both batches are sufficiently pulled they can be lightly pulled together just before cutting. You can also try moulding your roll of pulled toffee round scraps of chocolate to make satin cushions.

The only real trick in making humbugs is to learn by the feel of the pulled toffee when it is beginning to lose its pliability. If it sets before you have finished cutting your humbugs you still have a delectable sweet, but if you think how long it takes toffee to set you will realize that you have plenty of time if you work reasonably quickly.

Honey Balls

¼ lb candied peel, chopped
¼ lb glacé cherries
¼ lb dates, stoned and chopped
Warmed clear liquid honey to mix
Chopped walnuts

Mix peel, cherries and dates, adding enough warmed honey to bind them together. Form into little balls or logs and roll them in the chopped walnuts until covered. Place on a wire rack to dry out.

Alternatives to chopped walnuts: a mixture of cocoa and icing sugar, or chocolate vermicelli.

Honeycomb Toffee

2 oz white sugar
4 oz clear liquid honey
1 tsp bicarbonate of soda

Boil sugar and honey until the colour is deep golden brown. While still boiling add bicarbonate of soda, stirring it in very quickly. Pour into a shallow, well-greased tin. When almost firm slide a greased knife round the edges to loosen toffee from the tin and turn it out on to a wire rack to cool. When quite cold break into small pieces by tapping with a knife or toffee hammer.

Vienna Nuts

Take about 3 dozen nuts (brazils, halved walnuts, almonds). Make honey butterscotch and when it is nearly ready bring about 1 inch of water to the boil in a frying pan. When the butterscotch is ready place the saucepan in the frying pan so that the water (which must be just below boiling point) keeps the butterscotch from cooling.

Drop the nuts a few at a time into the butterscotch, fishing them out with a spoon and laying them out, not touching, on waxed paper. Leave to cool and wrap in waxed paper if you intend to keep them for later.

Honey Marzipan

Like many other things that we remember as glorious, marzipan, that traditional and rich confection, is not what it was. This is because almost invariably soy flour is substituted for ground almonds and we are left with a sweetish paste. You can never get the true marzipan taste with soy flour, even if you add almond essence. And, as the older and more dictatorial cookbooks would say, when making *proper* marzipan, let the almonds be freshly ground.

1½ oz butter
2 oz icing sugar
1 tbs clear liquid honey
4 oz freshly ground almonds
Vanilla essence to taste
Water to mix if necessary

Mix butter, sugar and honey in a saucepan, bringing them slowly to the boil. Cool a little, add ground almonds and vanilla essence (and a little water if necessary) to make a very stiff paste. Turn out on to a board and knead hard and well until it is pliable and free from cracks.

Marzipan Fruits

These confections were once very much in fashion, and a box of them still makes one of the nicest presents for elderly relatives, not only because marzipan fruits bring back pleasant memories of the past but because the gift indicates that time and care has been spent in making them. They also add a traditional touch to dinner-party decorations.

Making marzipan fruits can be considered either fascinating or tedious, according to your temperament. If you find them tedious this is not a recipe for you, because they can be rather time-consuming.

Shape your marzipan while it is still warm and pliable into the shape of various fruits—strawberries, bananas, apples and oranges are the most usual. In defiance of nature all fruits are made approximately the same size, about 1-1½ in in diameter.

Impale your piece of fruit on a long pin inserted where you will later be placing the stalk. The ideal pin is of course a hat pin. (It's a pity they've gone out of fashion, but they can usually be bought in Oxfam shops!)

Paint the surface of the fruit with culinary dye of the appropriate colour, drying completely in between coats.

When the fruit achieves the right depth of colour embellish it with the characteristics of the different fruits—pips on strawberries, red cheeks on apples, a few brown spots on bananas.

Make a few leaves and strawberry hulls by cutting the shapes out of coarse green cotton material and stiffening them with size (bought from a hardware shop) or colourless liquid glue. Make stalks by taking a small length of fine wire and wrapping the sized or glued material round it. Lay your leaves or strawberry hulls on top of the fruit and skewer them into place with the stalk.

Marzipan Eggs

It is also quite possible to make Easter eggs, now a horribly expensive item, from marzipan. The proper moulds are not easy to buy these days, but small solid marzipan eggs can be made by hand, while hollow eggs can be made in two halves, using anything egg-shaped as a mould (even a real egg if you handle it carefully) with the edges of the two halves glued together with white of egg. These eggs can be decorated with piped icing in various colours. Children always like to see their names on Easter eggs.

Marzipan Icing for Cakes

Dust board and rolling pin with icing sugar and roll out the marzipan until it is about ¼ in thick. Spread the marzipan with apricot jam (with which it has an affinity) and place it, jam side down, on the cake. Press firmly.

Preserves and Spreads

Honey Butter

2 level tbs clear liquid honey
8 oz soft butter

Beat honey and butter until quite smooth and very creamy. Use as a spread or cake filling.

Lemon Honey Butter

½ lb honey butter
1 tbs lemon juice
Grated peel of 1 lemon

Beat the lemon juice into the honey butter and then beat in grated peel.

Orange Honey Butter

As for lemon honey butter, but substituting orange juice and grated peel.

Spiced Honey Butter

½ lb honey butter
¼ tsp grated nutmeg
¼ tsp grated cinnamon
¼ tsp allspice

Beat spices into honey butter.

Ginger Honey Butter

½ lb honey butter
1 tbs chopped crystallized ginger

Beat chopped ginger into honey butter.

Mint Honey Butter

½ lb honey butter
1 tbs chopped fresh mint

Beat chopped mint into honey butter.

Rose Petal Jam

This has always been considered a luxury and something of a curiosity, extremely fashionable in Victorian times but used only on special occasions. The rose petals must be fresh, gathered as soon as the blooms begin to overblow; this means careful watching and a certain amount of spoilage of rose bushes. But it tastes of the scent of roses and of the memory of lovely summers. Eating it is a nostalgic ceremony.

1 lb fresh rose petals (preferably dark red)
½ lb white sugar
½ lb clear liquid honey
1 pt of water
Few drops crimson colouring
Juice of 1 lemon
Commercial pectin

Chop the petals, snipping off and discarding the thick bases. Cook very gently in the water until tender (about 10 minutes). Strain and use the water with the sugar and honey to make a syrup, boiling for 10 minutes. Add the rose petals and simmer very gently for 40 minutes, stirring occasionally. Add lemon juice and pectin; continue simmering until a drop sets immediately on a plate. Add a few drops of red colouring.

Honey Curd

3 egg whites
4 egg yolks
½ pt clear liquid honey
½ lb fresh butter
Juice and grated peel of 2 lemons

Mix the ingredients until the egg-whites are well mixed in. Place in the top of a double boiler and cook over the slowest possible heat until the mixture thickens. Pour immediately into warm jars and seal.

Store in a cool place. Honey curd should keep for at least a year.

Pickles and Relishes

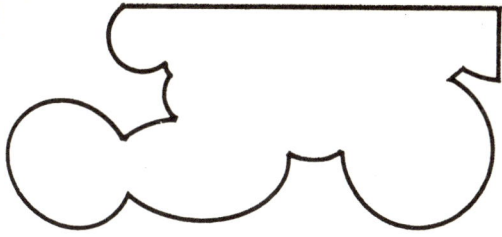

I always think that pickles and relishes are the better for the addition of a little honey, as this reduces the harshness of the vinegar. Obviously the more honey you add, the sweeter your pickle will be.

An additional word about vinegar: don't forget that no matter what other ingredients your pickles contain, vinegar is the basis, and no pickle will be better in quality than the quality of the vinegar you use. So a harsh vinegar will give you a harsh pickle. Although good-quality wine or cider vinegars may be expensive, it is a false economy to cut your costs in this direction. " Bought pickle " is rapidly losing public popularity because acetic acid is increasingly substituted for properly made vinegar. It would be a great pity if you went to the trouble of making your own pickles only to get this same burning tartness in your home-made product.

Pickled Red Cabbage

Take the outside leaves off a red cabbage, cut it into quarters, cut out the stem and slice cabbage finely. Sprinkle lavishly with salt and leave for 24 hours, then drain off the brine.

Boil up 1 qt vinegar with 1 tbs honey, ½ oz peppercorns, 1 oz bruised root ginger and a little allspice. Pack the cabbage into jars and pour the strained vinegar over. Cover and seal.

Dill Pickle

Cucumbers and dill have a complete affinity and although you will always get a better pickle if fresh dill is used, dill seed makes a reasonable substitute. This recipe calls for small fresh cucumbers, 4 to 5 in in length. Larger cucumbers can be used, in which case they should be sliced or diced.

14 small cucumbers
6 oz salt
1 gal boiling water
1 gal vinegar
1 tbs dill seed
1 tsp tarragon leaves
1 onion, cut into small slivers
1 red pimento, cut into small slivers
6 crushed peppercorns
Few caraway seeds
Couple of chillies
8 fl oz clear liquid honey

Soak the cucumbers in the boiling brine for 24 hours, placing a plate or saucer on top of them to keep them immersed. Drain them, place them in a dry bowl and cover them with boiling vinegar. Strain off the vinegar and boil it up again with the addition of the honey. Pour it over the cucumbers again. Leave for at least 12 hours, then remove the cucumbers and pack them into jars with the other ingredients. Boil up the vinegar again and pour it into the packed jars and seal.

Leave for at least a week before using.

Pickled Walnuts

Walnuts should be ready for pickling in July, and are used green and unhusked. They are suitable only if you can pass a large darning needle through them, because if the shells have started to form you will get unpleasant hard pieces in your pickle.

Bruise the nuts and cover them with well salted vinegar, leaving them for 3 days. Remove them from the vinegar and place them on wire racks to dry in the sun until they turn black. Pack into warmed jars.

Boil up some good quality vinegar with a bay leaf, mace, peppercorns and tarragon sprigs, and 1 tbs clear liquid honey to each pint. Strain and reboil. While still hot pour over the walnuts. Cover, seal and keep for a month or two before using.

Serve with fried fish, cold meat or as a garnish for braised steak.

Prune Pickle

1 lb prunes
4 blades mace
2 dozen cloves
½ tsp allspice
Few peppercorns
½ tsp salt
1 tbs clear liquid honey
½ pt good-quality vinegar

Wash the prunes and place them in a pan with the mace, cloves, allspice, peppercorns and salt. Cover with water and simmer for 2 hours, topping up with water if necessary. Add the honey and simmer for 10 minutes more, stirring to dissolve the honey. Add vinegar and boil rapidly for 5 minutes. Pot in warm jars and seal.

Serve with any type of cold meat. Especially good with cold lamb. The rich fruity taste also makes it a fine accompaniment to a hot curry.

Pickled Onions

Choose small pickling onions, preferably those with silvery skins. Take off the papery outer skin and the one below it, then cover the onions with boiling brine. Cool, drain and add fresh brine. Drain again and place the onions in jars, covering with vinegar that has been simmered for half an hour with 1 tsp honey, 1 tsp black pepper, a slice or two of ginger and a blade of mace to each pint. Cover and seal.

Tomato Relish

1 lb tomatoes
1 cooking apple
2 sticks celery
5 gherkins
4 tbs olive oil
2 tbs malt vinegar
1 tsp salt
½ level tsp dry mustard
1 tsp clear liquid honey
Few drops hot chilli sauce

Cover tomatoes with boiling water, leave for about a minute, then drain, peel and chop. Peel, core and chop apple, slice celery and gherkins and mix with tomatoes. Mix other ingredients well and add to mixture, stirring until well coated. Leave for an hour before serving. Keeps for about a week under refrigeration.
Note: The attraction of this relish is the fresh taste and crunchy texture of the raw apples and celery. If all the ingredients are cooked until soft it makes an excellent " keeping " relish, which can be potted and kept.

Index of Recipes

Dressings
Cole Slaw Dressing	54
Garlic Yoghurt Dressing	15
Honey Dressing	53
Honey Mayonnaise	53
Mayonnaise Aspic	53
Plain Yoghurt Dressing	15
Russian Dressing	15
Vinaigrette	53
Yoghurt and Honey Dressing	15
Yoghurt Mayonnaise	16

Sauces
Barbecue	15
Bearnaise	15
Bechamel	15
Chilli	15
Horseradish	15
Soubise	15
Tartare	14

Dips
Avocado	43
Bargee	43
Crazy Maisie	43
Dipsea Dip	43
Curry	16
Garlic	17
Liptaeur Cheese	43
Plum and Carrot	16
Pugaree	43
Strawberry	16
Tomato	16
Waldorf	16
White Russian	43

Starters
Aztec	45
Cheesy Apples	44
Coupe Caprice	18
Cream Cheese Omelette	45
Creamy Crab Pancakes	44
Devilled Ham Spread	45
Eggs Florentine	18
Eggs in Jelly	18
Kipper Cole Slaw	54
Lemon Crab	54
Pears Vinaigrette	54
Prawns Vol-au-Vent	18
Sherried Grapefruit	54
Shrimp Mousse	45
Stuffed Eggs	45
Waldorf Slaw	17
Yoghurt Mousse	18

Soups
Apple and Wine	21
Borscht	19
Chicken Avocado	19
Clear Tomato	28
Curry and Apple	21
Curry and Rice	21
Jajik	19
Orange	21
Peanut Butter	20
Watercress	20

Fish
Baked Coley Fillets	30
Cod en Papillote	29
Crab Casserole	30
Haddock Quiche	46

Index

Kipperee	31	Tuna	57
Orange Plaice	31		
Plaice Duxelle	29	**Side Salads**	
Russian Haddock	30	Cucumber	58
Salmon Loaf	46	Orange and Watercress	58
Salmon Puff	46	Pineapple	58
Tuna Casserole with Cashew Nuts	31	Potato	58
Tuna and Cucumber Flan	30	Tomato and Basil	58

Poultry

		Vegetables	
Bechamel Chicken, German Style	22	Broad Beans à la Turque	35
Chicken and Potato Pie	23	Broccoli in Yoghurt Sauce	34
Chicken Soufflé	23	Cabbage	35
Creamed Chicken	23	Crudities	16
Game Hens	24	French Beans with Pears	35
Honey Duck	55	Green Beans and Almonds	34
Indian Boiled Chicken	24	Jacket Potatoes	34
Stuffed Marrow	24	Polish Beetroot	34
Tandoori Chicken	25	Salsify	34
Turkey Club Sandwich	23	Stuffed Green Peppers	35
Turkey Supreme	22		

		Desserts	
Meat		Apple Strudel	37
Barbecue Pork Chops	23	Apple Ratafia	40
Boeuf Stroganoff	25	Apple Snow	40
Colonial Goose	56	Apricot Fritters	40
Baked Gammon with		Baked Apples	59
Orange/Honey Glaze	56	Baked Honey Custard	60
Honey-Glazed Bacon	56	Battered Bananas	60
Indian Pillau	26	Butterscotch Sundae	60
Kidneys à la Turque	27	Charlotte Russe	39
Lamb Chop Skillet	25	Cheesecake	47
Lamb Kebabs	28	Cheesecake, cherry	48
Liver with Yoghurt and Sherry	28	Cheesecake, orange	48
Moussaka	26	Cheesecake, rum and raisin	48
Oslo Chops	28	Fruit Melange	41
Turkish Lamb	27	Fruit Yoghurt	41
		Hazelnut and Apple Yoghurt	41
Main-Course Salads		Heart of Cream	48
Capri	57	Indian Carrot Pudding	39
Chicken	33	Malvern Pudding	59
Chicken Mould	32	Melba Cocktail	40
Cucumber Jelly	33	Mint Yoghurt	41
Dandelion	58	Oranges Romanesque	41
Danish Herring	32	Pancakes	38
Flower Garden	58	Pancakes, Ambrosia	38
Kipper Cole Slaw	54	Pancakes, Melba	38
Nicoise	57	Pancakes, Orange	38
Shrimp Loaf	33	Pavlova	36
Smoked Haddock	33	Peaches Royale	60
Spinach	33	Strawberries Antigua	36
Stuffed Egg	32	Strawberry Sherbet	41

Index

Tipsy Yoghurt	41
Witchcraft Cake	38

Bread and Cakes

Chocolate Honey Cookies	63
Fairings	63
Flat Bread	61
Honey Fruit Bread	61
Honey Ginger Cake	61
Mockeroons	63
Petits-Fours	62

Sweets

Fudge, Basic Honey	64
Fudge, Cherry Walnut	64
Fudge, Chocolate	64
Fudge, Coffee	64
Fudge, Ginger	64
Fudge, Rum and Raisin	64
Honey Balls	66
Honey Butterscotch	65
Honey Humbugs	65
Honey Popcorn	64
Honeycomb Toffee	66
Marzipan	66
Marzipan Eggs	67
Marzipan Fruits	66
Marzipan Icing	67
Vienna Nuts	66

Spreads

Honey Butter	67
Honey Butter, Ginger	67
Honey Butter, Lemon	67
Honey Butter, Mint	67
Honey Butter, Orange	67
Honey Butter, Spiced	67
Honey Curd	67
Rose Petal Jam	67

Pickles and Relishes

Dill Pickle	69
Pickled Onions	70
Pickled Red Cabbage	69
Pickled Walnuts	70
Prune Pickle	70
Tomato Relish	70

Drinks

Coonardoo	42
Yoghurt Shakes	42

Notes

Notes

Notes

Notes

Notes